The Seven Ages of Man

THE
SEVEN
AGES
OF MAN

EDITED BY
Robert R. Sears
S. Shirley Feldman

WILLIAM KAUFMANN, INC.
Los Altos, California

Library of Congress Cataloging in Publication Data
Main entry under title:

The Seven ages of man.

Originally published in 1964 as a 7-part series in
New society.
 Bibliography: p.
 1. Developmental biology. 2. Developmental
psychology. 3. Aging. I. Sears, Robert Richardson,
1908– ed. II. Feldman, S. Shirley, ed.
[DNLM: 1. Child development. 2. Personality
development. BF698 S497 1973]
QP84.6.S48 1973   612.6   73–12029
ISBN 0–913232–07–6
ISBN 0–913232–06–8 (pbk.)

Originally published as a series of articles in the
magazine NEW SOCIETY, 128 Long Acre, London WC2E 9QH,
England. Reprinted here with some adaptations with
their permission.

Printed in the United States of America.

1 2 3 4 5 6 7 8 9

Introduction

There has been for too long a troublesome myth in our scientific lore that *development* is something which happens only to children. Most books on human development start with the embryo, carry the story on informatively through late adolescence, and then wish the unfinished product farewell and godspeed.

Growth and change are dramatic in the first two decades of life, to be sure. But the next five or six decades are every bit as complex and important, not only to those adults who are passing through them but to their children, who must live with and understand parents and grandparents. The changes in body, personality and abilities through these later decades are very great. There are severe developmental tasks imposed by marriage and parenthood, by the waxing and waning of physical prowess and of some (but not all) intellectual capacities, by the children's flight from the nest, by the achievement of an occupational plateau, and by the facing of retirement and the prospect of final extinction. By and large, people accomplish these tasks. Some do it more gracefully and effectively than others, and there is no denying the uniqueness of every personality. But the very nature of human growth, coupled with the commonality of human experience in a given culture, is reflected in the considerable similarity among age-mates in the adjustment problems they suffer and the particular personality qualities they develop at various ages. Parents have always been fascinated by their children's development, but it is high time adults began to look objectively at themselves, to examine the systematic changes in their own physical, mental and emotional qualities, as they pass through the life cycle, and to get acquainted with the limitations and assets they share with so many others of their own age.

The Seven Ages of Man provides a balanced, accurate and revealing portrayal of human development from infancy to old age. It was prepared by a number of British specialists in developmental biology and psychology for publication as a series of seven installments in *New Society*, a journal published weekly in London. The title of the original series, and of this book, obviously was suggested by the famous lines from William Shakespeare's comedy, "As You Like It" (Act II, Scene VII):

> All the world's a stage,
> And all the men and women merely players.
> They have their exits and their entrances,
> And one man in his time plays many parts,
> His acts being seven ages . . .

The seven installments appear in this book as chapters, each consisting of three sections. The first presents the anatomical and physiological characteristics of that particular age span and the changes that occur during it. The second describes some of the similarities and variations in personality, feelings, motives and emotional problems that characterize that age. The third describes the changes in abilities associated with that part of the life cycle and applies these facts to an understanding of social, educational or occupational roles and problems. The division of the book into ages and topical areas is for expository convenience only; the authors make abundantly clear the continuity of human life from one phase to the next and the dependence of each aspect of development on every other.

In editing and updating the original material for publication in book form, we have substituted United States census data for British data where this seemed appropriate. We have also added a number of simple charts to give perspective on certain physical and social changes that have occurred over the last century; any one person's life cycle is lived out in a specific historical time, and times change. Occasionally we have inserted editorial notes in the text to expand on points that seemed to deserve it, or to add information coming from more recent American research. Some of these notes refer the reader to specific bibliographic references found in the list of supplementary readings at the end of the book. We hope this annotated list will provide an easy means for readers to pursue their particular interests further and for students in various disciplines to find their way into discussions of specific topics at greater depth.

Robert R. Sears
S. Shirley Feldman

Stanford University
October 1, 1973

Contents

The Seven Ages of Man

PART ONE

Infancy: 0 to 5 years

*In the first five years dramatic changes occur
in physical, cognitive and emotional development. Socialization proceeds
more rapidly at this stage than at any other.*

Chapter 1

THE BODY

W. A. MARSHALL
Lecturer in Growth and Development
London University

If we watch a group of 5 year olds at play, we recognize immediately many of the characteristics which we associate with ourselves and other human beings. They walk and run on two legs, they talk, they are capable of quite skilled activities with their hands. They are obviously fully conscious of their surroundings and are capable of quite complicated thought and emotion. None of these things can be said of newborn babies.

A very young baby is not only smaller than a 5 year old, it is quite a different shape. About a quarter of its total length of between 18 and 22 inches is due to the head, while the remainder is divided equally between the trunk and the limbs. The stature of 5 year olds varies between 40 and 47 inches, but only about one-eighth of this is head, while the legs form more than half of the remainder. These changes in proportion continue a process which began in the mother's uterus. The head of the fetus grows very quickly, while the trunk lags behind and the legs grow even more slowly. Growth

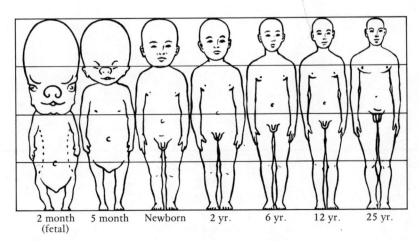

| 2 month
(fetal) | 5 month | Newborn | 2 yr. | 6 yr. | 12 yr. | 25 yr. |

FIGURE 1. Changes in body form and proportion during fetal and post-natal life. From C. M. Jackson. Some aspects of form and growth. In W. J. Robbins, S. Brody, A. F. Hogan, C. M. Jackson and C. W. Green. *Growth.* New Haven: Yale University Press, 1928, p. 118.

of the head is nearly complete by the end of the second year of life and then slows down markedly, while the trunk grows quickly. The most rapid growth of all is in the legs.

Because of the immaturity of the brain at birth, the newborn is only aware of his environment to a limited extent, and his means of responding to it are even more limited. Consciousness, as we think of it, probably does not exist in the newborn, but the sense of pain does; and the baby is also sensitive to touch and pressure, which initiate such responses as sucking and grasping with the hand. Some sensations of warmth and cold are present, and a sense of taste is sufficiently well-developed to distinguish sweet from salty, bitter and sour substances. The responses to all these sensations are, however, of purely reflex character and are mediated by the parts of the central nervous system below the level of the cerebral cortex.

The newborn child is unable to fix his eyes on objects, although the eyes themselves are fully formed and the eyelids and pupils react to stimulation by light. [EDITORS' NOTE: *Despite this, the infant is able to distinguish form with remarkably good acuity at birth* (See Mussen, Conger & Kagen, Chap. 5).]

The ability to fix objects appears between the third and fifth months when the primary visual area of the cerebral cortex, which is the receiving center for visual impressions, has developed considerably. Even at this age the visual association area, where the recognition and identification of objects takes place, is not developed to an extent which would permit the baby to interpret its visual sensations. [EDITORS' NOTE: *Recent evidence on the infant's recognition of mother's face—one of the most familiar objects in the infant's environment—suggests that by 4–6 weeks of age there is rudimentary recognition of the mother, as expressed by greater attention and more vocalizing to the mother than to a stranger.*]

Most newborn infants will respond to certain noises, and some will even turn their heads toward the source of sound, but they do not usually do this until about the seventh month.

By 15 months the part of the brain which controls the movement of the eyes is well developed and so is the visual association area, so that the baby can probably attach some significance to what he sees. At 2 years the auditory association area is less far advanced than the visual one, so that there is probably less discriminative ability in hearing than in vision. Color vision is well developed by the age of 3 months and probably some time before this.

The movement of muscles is controlled by nerve cells in the spinal cord. Whenever one of these cells becomes active, it passes an electrical impulse to the muscle fibers with which it is connected, causing them to contract. A large number of nerve cells acting in this way causes whole muscles or groups of muscles to contract and move the appropriate part of the body. The activity of each of these spinal "motor" cells is controlled by impulses coming from groups of cells in various parts of the brain and spinal cord. These cell groups are known as "motor centers" and are interconnected in such a way that they influence each other's activity. The balance between the effect of those centers which tend to produce movement and those which tend to prevent it is under the overall control of the motor area of the cerebral cortex, which controls voluntary movement by adjusting this balance. This part of the cortex is just as immature at birth as those parts concerned with sensation and its interpretation. The pattern of movements seen in newborn babies is, therefore, the same as that found in malformed infants who are born without cerebral hemispheres. After the first two or three weeks of life these movements, which are initiated by a primitive motor center, are gradually inhibited by higher centers as these develop. Later, as the motor area of the cerebral cortex and its connections mature, voluntary movements become possible. After one month there is considerable evidence of maturation in the motor cortex, particularly those areas concerned with the movements of the upper limbs and trunk.

Independent locomotion develops in a series of definite stages during the first year. First of all there is development of the mechanism which enables the baby to position his head correctly in space while he is lying on his abdomen. He next begins to creep, using only his arms, and then to crawl, using his legs as well. He may then slide about on his buttocks before developing an erect gait. Individual infants may omit one or another of these stages. The cerebellum, which plays a major part in the coordination of movement and the control of posture, grows more than any other part of the brain during the first two and a half years after birth.

No amount of teaching or practice will cause a baby to walk or perform any other skilled act before the necessary mechanisms in the nervous system are mature. When the neural pathways have developed, the skills will follow. Similarly voluntary control of the bowels and bladder cannot be developed by training before the necessary degree of maturity has been reached, and this may be much later in some babies than in others.

The reflexes of a newborn infant are entirely unconditioned, but the ability to form conditioned reflexes increases rapidly during the early months of life. Conditioned reflexes in response to words do not appear until after the first year, so that attempts to teach babies under about 15 months to obey commands are generally fruitless. [EDITORS' NOTE: *Other evidence suggests considerably younger children are able to respond to words. For example, actions to words— such as pat-a-cake, waving bye-bye—occur during the last few months of the first year. At about 12 months the infant obeys simple commands* (Gesell and Thompson).]

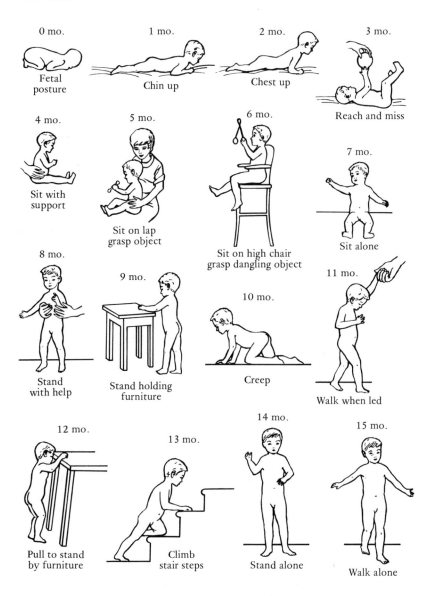

FIGURE 2. Sequence of motor development and locomotion in infants. From Shirley, M. M. *The First Two Years: Vol. II. Intellectual Development.* Minneapolis: Universtiy of Minnesota Press, 1933, copyright renewed, 1961.

Very little is known about the growth of the brain after the second year of life, but it is clear from the child's increasing control of his movements that some development continues in the motor centers and pathways at least until the age of 4. It has not yet been possible to demonstrate physical changes in the brain which would account for the continuing development of the intellect after this age.

During infancy most of the internal organs grow in proportion to the rest of the body, so that the lungs, heart, kidneys and so on are well able to cope with the demands placed upon them by the rapidly increasing size of the child as a whole.

The tonsils and adenoids grow very rapidly in early life, and by the end of the fifth year they are the same size as in the adult. The presence of these large masses of tissue in the small throat and nasopharynx of the infant may lead to blockage of the eustachian tube which connects this region with the middle ear and so plays an important part in producing the ear infections which are so common in infancy and may cause permanent impairment of hearing.

The food and water requirements of children decrease in relation to body weight during the first five years of life, as might be expected from the fact that the overall rate of growth is also decreasing steadily during this period. Severe malnutrition will delay physical development, but if a malnourished child is given an adequate diet, it will usually grow more rapidly than normal until it catches up with older children, who have always been well fed. Only prolonged malnutrition has a permanent effect on growth. Similarly prolonged severe illness may seriously impair growth, but there is no convincing evidence that either minor illness or minor variations in diet can have any permanent effect. If a child is unusually small in spite of an adequate diet, nothing will be gained by trying to "feed him up," as his shortness is most likely to be the result of some fault in his endocrine glands, an inherited abnormality, or some chronic disease which has not yet been recognized. The treatment of abnormally short stature is therefore a task for the physician and not the cook.

The average 5 year old has not only grown to a little more than twice the size he was when he was born, but he has changed in shape so that his general proportions are much more like those of the adult. The basic nervous mechanisms of sensation, understanding and the voluntary control of movement have all fully developed so that the baby, which was less developed at birth than the young of most farm animals, has become unmistakably human.

Chapter 2

PERSONALITY

ANTHONY AMBROSE
The Tavistock Institute of Human Relations
London

The personality of an individual consists of the characteristic ways in which he relates to other people, meets his own needs and desires as well as theirs, copes with frustration and stress, and feels about himself. There is no period in life quite as crucial for personality formation as the first five years. On the one hand, the basic patterns developed by that age endure, subject to modification only in detail, to influence all later development. On the other, in this early period of crystallization the child is at its most vulnerable to influences that make the difference between mental health and mental illness, and which affect the particular form taken by either.

Thus vulnerability stems from a number of unique features of this period of life: the intensity of the child's dependence upon and attachment to his mother and other family members; his limited capacity to tolerate frustration and stress; his limited understanding of causes and effects; and the very high rate at which he has to adjust to entirely new experiences which result from his rapidly expanding capacities, skills and desires.

Development over these early years normally entails rapid and fundamental changes in perception, emotion and behavior. From a state of virtual nonawareness the infant develops a distinction between self and others. His horizon of other people expands from mere parts of the mother, to the mother as an individual person, to the father and siblings, and sooner or later to persons outside the family such as playmates, nursery teachers, and television personalities. From total dependence he gradually moves, in spite of setbacks, towards independence of feeling, thought and action. His demands for immediate satisfaction give way to toleration of delay in satisfaction. Desires, interests, attitudes, values and taboos increasingly conform to the culture represented by the family into which he is born, first through external sanctions but later through internal control.

Our conceptions of the forces that mould an individual into a unique personality are at last becoming free of the false assumptions of the old nature-nurture controversy. Just as the area of a rectangle is fully dependent upon both its length and its breadth, so developing emotional and social behavior depends upon both inheritance and environment. Maturation can occur at all only under appropriate environmental conditions, and learning can occur only by virtue of genetically determined structure and process.

As a result, several related principles are now guiding research on the determinants of personality. First, at all phases of development, maturation will be fostered or hampered by the nature of the prevailing environment, whether intra-uterine, physical or social. For instance, prolonged maternal deprivation, under extreme institutional conditions, can lead to severely retarded development. Second, because the cognitive, emotional and behavioral capacities of the growing child change so radically with development, a given aspect of the environment may be of the highest significance at one phase but of none at another. An angry facial expression may be meaningless at 2 months but a powerful influence at 2 years.

Third, favorable development requires an environment which is appropriate to the needs and capacities characteristic of any phase, yet still allows for differences between individuals. Psychological disturbance arises from persistent interaction with the environment that is inappropriate either to phase or individual. For example, the child of 3 months requires much more cuddling than a child of 3 years, but either too much or too little of it can lead to emotional disturbance. Fourth, the type of disturbance set up will vary both with the kind of interactional failure involved and with the phase of development at which it occurs. Because the character of an individual at any phase is the outcome of development through previous ones, upset or deficiency in one phase will increase the chance of failures in adjustment in later ones. For example, obsessional neurosis seems to be particularly linked to difficulties at the phase of toilet training.

This outlook on development reveals how the formation of personality over the early years is affected by many different kinds of factors. The earliest influences, even within the womb, are not wholly genetic. Severe anxiety or emotional upset in the pregnant mother has biochemical effects on the growing fetus which can lead to the newborn being unduly susceptible to stress; it can also lead to premature birth which, if extreme, increases the chances both of birth injury and also of illness in the early years. Immediately after birth, prolonged delay in breathing may retard subsequent development. Following birth, the establishment of effective feeding is greatly influenced by the shape of the nipple which, if not optimal, can result in difficulty in sucking. The establishment of stable breathing and gastro-intestinal functioning during the earliest weeks is made easier by mothers who fondle and talk to their babies appropriately. Indeed, recent animal research strongly suggests that early handling may have long-term effects on the emotional stability of the individual: for example, there is evidence that rats handled, even briefly, during infancy show greater resistance to stress later on than those which were not handled.

From the earliest feeding and handling onwards, a mother has an unremitting influence upon her child's developing personality through the techniques, attitudes and feelings with which she undertakes her maternal role. To the dawning awareness of her baby they will determine the balance between gratifying and stressful experiences. Over the first few months, as he forms his earliest impressions of what the world around him is like, it is the nature of this balance that gives rise to his feeling, either that it is basically benign and to be trusted, or that it is hostile and unreliable. The same applies to his emerging feelings about himself as he relates to his mother through sucking, crying, smiling and making sounds and spontaneous movements. If she responds to these warmly and rewardingly, he will come to feel that he is loved and acceptable and his self-expression will expand accordingly. But if her reaction to him is cool, stunted or even resentful and rejecting, then he will come to feel unaccepted, to distrust his own impulses, and the foundations of self-confidence will be missing.

These impressions are already well advanced when, by about 6 months, the baby becomes fully able to recognize his mother as a specific person from whom others are distinct. In the months and years that follow they are reinforced or modified, not only by her, but increasingly by the father and siblings as well. By learning from the ways they respond to him, by identifying with them as models, and by finding ways of coping with the thwartings and conflicts that inevitably confront him, he gradually forms his own particular pattern of adjustment to family life and to himself. Family atmosphere greatly affects this. In general, a warm and permissive one fosters a spontaneous and outgoing child, a cool and impersonal one results in a frustrated, anxious and inhibited child, and an overprotective and possessive one leads to an excessively dependent child.

Right up to the fifth year the mother usually remains the central feature of the child's environment. Her frequent closeness to him is vital, not just for what she can provide for him, but because she comprises a base from which he can explore and adjust to new people and things as they appear on his rapidly widening horizon. How he approaches and responds to them is largely determined by the pattern of his relation with his mother. If his attachment to her is secure and allows full expression of his developing capacities, he will be positive towards others and eager for new experiences. But if this attachment is full of frustration and anxiety, his relation to others is likely to be characterized by timidity and inhibition, which often conceal pent-up aggressive feelings. When he gets to nursery school, the quality of this attachment will be reflected not only by the way he relates to other children and to the teacher, but also by the form and content of his play and painting, and by his readiness to learn.

There is no hard and fast dividing line between normal and abnormal personality functioning. The many forms of each represent different methods of dealing with the impulses and conflicts which the individual brings to his relations with other people and things. The mentally healthy 5 year old has succeeded in establishing an internal organization in which loving, sexual, aggressive and depressive feelings can all contribute to his experience without undue anxiety and guilt. Mental illness, on the other hand, consists either of failure of some aspects of the personality to develop or of regression to modes of coping that were appropriate only at an earlier phase. These may result either from serious deficiencies in the child's social interactions, whether due to organic abnormality or parental failure, or from stress that has been excessive in relation to the child's capacity for withstanding it at any particular phase. Fixation to primitive coping methods results in hopelessly inadequate, or even culturally unacceptable, forms of personality functioning.

The development of a healthy personality is based, above all, on continuous mutual adjustment and readjustment between parents and the growing child. Because each of them have their own unique constellation of needs, capacities and shortcomings, this can never be wholly adequate. But as long as it is sufficient, its very incompleteness gives the necessary opportunity to a child to develop the capacity to tolerate frustration and to love others in spite of their limitations. This capacity is a hallmark of maturity, but a child can achieve it only if his parents themselves possess it and apply it to him first.

Chapter 3

ABILITY

B. M. FOSS
Lecturer in Psychology
Birkbeck College, London

It is difficult to think of the newborn child as having any abilities at all. He appears to be a bundle of reflexes, some dominated by physical needs of internal origin, such as hunger and the need to sleep, but some depending on the environment, for instance unpleasant stimuli or a drop in temperature which will promote crying. Yet by the age of 5, the child has already devloped a wide range of abilities and skills, and the individual differences between children are already clear cut. Five year olds differ from each other not only in general intelligence, but in verbal ability, in manual dexterity, in curiosity and imaginativeness of play, in perseverance at these things. John Stuart Mill was learning Greek at the age of 3, when at the other extreme, some handicapped children would still be reacting like newborn babies.

Such remarkable differences are the result of both genetic make-up and environmental influences, and without doubt, Mill was fortunate in both. There are still controversies over the relative parts played by heredity and environment. Several studies exist of identical twins (having the same genetic endowment) who are adopted by different families early in life. Despite being reared in very different environments, their intelligences as measured by IQ tests remain more alike than do those of fraternal twins reared in the same home. Apparently the effects of heredity on general intelligence are not fully seen until about the fifth year, because a recent study shows that the IQs of foster children become increasingly like those of their real parents up to that age, rather than like those of their foster parents.

The effects of environment are probably seen most in the special skills and interests which a child develops and in his use of language. The parental effect shows in all kinds of ways—in the rather obvious way in which the language development of the child depends on the extent to which the mother talks to him, but in more subtle ways too. For instance, there is evidence that the children of anxious parents are more likely to develop symbolic skills (such as the use of words) earlier, whereas the children of unanxious parents are likely to be better at manipulation and practical skills. Presumably their parents have allowed them to explore more.

The measurement of intelligence in young children poses several problems. Tests suitable for 5 year olds do begin to look like ordinary tests, and include questions on reasoning, short-term memory, spatial relations, the use of language and definitions. They include repeating a sentence of twelve syllables, drawing a man and defining common objects (like a fork, shoe or chair) in terms of their use. None of these is possible with the very young infant. The tests used during the first two years are derived from the supposed stages of development of simpler abilities—being able to follow with the eyes, to stand up, to name objects, identify parts of the body, build with blocks and so on. The measure is often called a development quotient rather than an intelligence quotient. The DQ measured during the first year does correlate significantly with the IQ measured in the early teens, but the correlation is not nearly high enough to enable prediction in individual cases. A child may appear below average at 1, but be well above average at 8.

What happens to a child in the first five years is powerful in determining skill and ability later. This importance of "early learning" is more easily demonstrated in animals. In some Canadian experiments, litters of puppies have been split, half being brought up as home pets, in what is described as a "rich environment", and half in "impoverished environments", enclosures which are visually dull, unresponsive, and with little to explore. Dogs reared in the dull environment for months, when compared with those reared in the home, were bad at solving problems and at learning how to cope with unpleasant stimuli. (Perhaps the Victorian drawing room packed with objects was a more stimulating environment than the stark, modern open plan!) The comparative lack of ability seemed long-lasting, and experiments of this kind have supported the idea that certain early experiences may affect later adaptability. (In one of the earliest experiments it was found that lambs raised with humans during the first days were "unsociable" when returned to the flock.)

In children, it is not clear which early experiences are likely to be the most potent, but there are studies which show that separation from the mother results in a depression of the development quotient, at least temporarily. [EDITORS' NOTE: *The quality of the substitute mothering and the nature of the separation (total or partial, short-term or long-term) are important determinants of the outcome. Children of the Kibbutz, raised by professional caretakers in group settings, but visited daily by their parents, show accelerated rather than depressed developmental quotients.* (For further information on Kibbutz child-rearing and its outcome see Rabin.) *While children in institutions show retardation in their development, it is not known whether this is due to separation from the mother* per se, *or to other environmental deprivations (such as impoverished sensory and social stimulation).*] It is still less clear which experiences have a more lasting effect on ability. It has been assumed that some kinds of learning have to occur in the early years if they are to develop at all efficiently. The learning of language was thought to be like this, but there are cases which show that language can be learned for the first time much later in life.

Until language has developed, the skills of a child resemble those of a chimpanzee (and are usually a bit slower) and are concerned with learning to control the body, to move about and explore and manipulate the environment. Why the child should develop language while the chimp does not (when reared with humans) is not known. It might be that the chimp has no appropriate speech mechanism, or no appropriate neural controls for it, or is bad at learning by imitation, or cannot develop the concepts needed for developing language (rather than just learning a vocabulary); or probably a combination of these.

Before a child can speak, he produces most of the noises which are needed for his language, and many others too. There follows a process of elimination in which phonemes which do not occur in the mother tongue drop out of the infant's babblings. (Some are relearned later only with great effort when the child is taught foreign languages.) Probably all vowel sounds are there in the prelingual babbling, but many of the consonants must be learned later.

Words and sentences are probably learned in a way not unlike other kinds of learning in animals and humans. If the child produces roughly the right word by chance, the parents will reinforce the child with all kinds of attentions, and the more so the more accurate the child is. This is a well-understood kind of learning through reinforcement. Probably straightforward imitation, without reinforcement, also occurs. When the child has acquired a sufficient vocabulary, he will spend much time playing with words, putting them in different combinations and sequences. [EDITORS' NOTE: *Recent research suggests that imitation and reinforcement cannot be considered entirely adequate to explain language learning, for the essence of human language is creativity in expressing meanings. However, there are constraints on the creativity of speech: to be intelligible to others, language must obey a set of rules which is shared by other speakers of that language. Even the earliest utterances show children are learning rule-systems which enable them to generate potential utterances as well as actual utterances. For example, the sentence "I goed home" shows that the child has learned the rule of forming a past-tense by adding "ed", rather than simply imitating an existing statement. (For further information on language learning and developmental psy-*

cholinguistics see the two books by Brown, *Words and Things*, and *Social Psychology*, Chaps. 6 & 7.)]

To the extent that he has learned that words stand for things, his language play carries with it experiments in meanings, the beginnings of verbal thinking. This in turn becomes quicker, more elliptical and sub vocal.

The most famous system concerned with the intelligent behavior of children is that devised by Jean Piaget, the Swiss psychologist, with his stages in which intelligent behavior develops. The stages even hold for the feeble-minded as well as more normal children.

These stages Piaget has organized into three periods: the sensori-motor period (0-2 years) during which the child progresses from a reflex level, in which he and his environment are undifferentiated from each other, to a state in which his sensori-motor adjustments to the world are well organized, but organized in a practical way to suit the immediate environment. There is as yet little thinking about the environment. The second period (2-11 years) is concerned with the preparation for and organization of concrete operations, and progresses from the earliest representational thinking to the beginnings of formal thought. In the final period (from about age 11) formal thought is possible, including abstractions, propositional statements and the world of "as if".

Each of these periods is divided into stages, during which the child adds to his cognitive development from previous stages. For instance, at the last stage of the sensori-motor period (at about 18 months) he will invent new methods of doing things not by overt trial and error, but covertly, thinking of possible solutions before trying them out.

One of Piaget's earliest and most useful concepts is that of egocentrism in thinking—an inability to see the world from anyone else's point of view. Egocentrism of most kinds extends well beyond the fifth year. A child is asked how many brothers he has. "Two, Paul and Henry." And how many brothers has Paul? "One, Henry." Not until 10 years of age were 75 per cent of children right on this kind of thing. For a child of 5, such egocentrism also applies to ideas of space. He cannot imagine what an object will look like from any point of view other than his own at the moment.

The child's progress from the mewling, puking infant to the whining schoolboy is shaped by his environment, yet gradually leads him to a growing independence of that environment. His solving of problems begins to be symbolic rather than manipulative, so that he is no longer a bundle of reflexes at the mercy of his environment; but he still shows, to a marked degree, an inability to see any viewpoint but his own.

PART TWO

Childhood: 6 to 12 years

*The second part of our survey
describes children in their elementary school years:
how they learn to live together, to categorize and
to make sense of some of their experiences.*

Chapter 4

THE BODY

W. A. MARSHALL
Lecturer in Growth and Development
London University

Between the ages of 5 and 8 years, children usually become bigger at a fairly constant rate and nothing very dramatic occurs; but between 8 and 12, events take place which are of tremendous importance to society as a whole, as well as to the children themselves. During these years, puberty begins in more than half the girls in the population and is completed by many of them. Some boys are also well advanced in puberty by the age of 12, but this stage of development in boys is more typical of the period considered in Chapter 5 and only girls' puberty will be considered in detail here. [EDITORS' NOTE: *In customary terminology puberty is distinguished from adolescence. Puberty refers to the period when the reproductive system matures. Adolescence is defined psycho-socially as the period of time following puberty and ending with the emotional and behavioral autonomy of adulthood.*]

Slight enlargement of the breasts and the appearance of pubic hair are the first signs of approaching sexual maturity, and these typically appear at the age of 11. In some early-developing girls these changes appear as young as 8 years of age, while other perfectly normal girls may have to wait until they are 13 or more before development occurs.

At about the same time as the first signs of sexual development appear, there is a generalized acceleration of growth known as the growth spurt. This affects the whole skeleton, even that of the head, which has grown very little since the first few years of life. The hips grow faster than the shoulders, so that they become relatively wider, producing the characteristic female body shape and making future childbearing easier. Shortly before the beginning of puberty the amount of fat on the limbs and the trunk begins to increase, and in girls this increase continues throughout and beyond the period of maturation, contributing further to the characteristically female curvature of the body contours.

The acceleration of growth in the limbs occurs before that of growth in the trunk, so that for a time the legs are relatively long. The trunk reaches its maximum rate of growth about a year after the limbs have passed theirs and is growing more quickly while the legs are slowing down.

The growth spurt also affects the muscles, causing an increase of strength, but this does not occur until the spurt in stature is well advanced. Thus many pubescent girls are not as strong as their size would suggest. All the abdominal organs enlarge, but those concerned with reproduction, the ovaries and uterus, do so more than the others.

The brain does not become noticeably bigger at this time, but there may well be an acceleration of structural changes within it, although very little is known about this as yet. The electroencephalogram suggests that some kind of change is taking place.

The tonsils, adenoids and other lymphoid tissues actually become smaller at the time of puberty and occupy a relatively much smaller proportion of the nasopharynx and throat; they therefore cease to be the potential nuisance that they were in infancy.

About a year or two after the growth spurt begins the rate of growth begins to decrease again, while development of the breasts and genitalia is completed. Menstruation does not begin until the period of most rapid growth has passed, and even then complete sexual maturity and fertility have not usually been attained, as the first cycles are not usually associated with the liberation of ova from the ovaries.

There is wide variation in the rates at which different girls approach maturity, so that some may have finished their pubescence and begun to menstruate regularly before others of the same age show any signs of development at all. But whether a girl matures early or late the same events take place in the same sequence. The beginning of sexual development is always associated with the beginning of the general growth spurt, and menstruation never begins until the greater part of the growth spurt is complete.

Because most girls have their growth spurt before most boys, girls at about the age of 11 are on the average both bigger and stronger than boys of the same age. Similarly, a girl who matures relatively early will, for a short time, be both bigger and stronger than her classmates in whom the growth spurt has not begun. She will also have the new interests and emotional problems which go along with adolescence.

These interests and problems have a special importance in modern society because there is irrefutable evidence from many parts of the world that girls are maturing at a progressively earlier age than they used to. The average age at which menstruation begins advances about four months every ten years, so that the typical girl of today may expect to menstruate when she is about ten months younger than her mother was at the beginning of her period. The average age at which menstruation begins in this country is now a little over 13 years, but the variation around this average is very great. Probably something between 10 and 20 per cent of girls now menstruate while they are still at primary school.

This raises immense social and moral problems. The fact that girls are maturing earlier does not only mean that they will be exposed to the sexual temptations of adulthood for a longer time before they can marry. The most important fact is that they are faced with the whole problem of adolescence at an age when they are far less equipped by education and general experience of life to deal with it than their mothers were. We all recognize that adolescence may

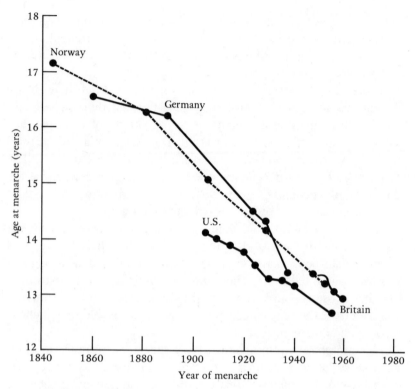

FIGURE 3. Decrease in age of menarche (first menstrual period) 1840–1960. From Tanner, J. M. Earlier maturation in man. Copyright © (1968) by Scientific American, Inc. All rights reserved.

cause a lot of disturbance, worry and even fear in a 12 or 13 year old. It must be very much more disturbing for an 8 or 9 year old, but it is seldom that any action is taken to help such a child to deal with her problems. If a girl's adolescence is to have a satisfactory outcome from either the personal or the social point of view, she must know beforehand, at least in a general sort of way, what sort of changes are going to take place in her body and her mind; with what sort of temptations she is going to be faced; and what harm may be done to herself or others if she yields to these temptations too soon.

The reason for this steady advance in the age at which physical maturity is reached is not clear. Possibly economic factors play a part; but these are unlikely to be the only factor, as all social classes are affected by the trend, although in England the effect is somewhat less marked in the well-off than in the poorer classes. It has been suggested that the increased sexual stimulation offered in modern society might be a cause, but there is no evidence to support this, and it has been shown that girls at coeducational schools do not menstruate any earlier than those in single sex schools. The average world temperature is rising steadily, but there is no evidence that a warmer climate has any effect on the age of menstruation. Eskimo and Nigerian girls begin to menstruate at about the same age, although it is possible that the difference between their diets may counteract some effect of the climate, which might have tended to produce a difference between the two groups. It is well-established that girls in small families menstruate at an earlier age than those in large ones, but the current trend toward smaller families is not sufficient to account for the general advancement of adolescence. A possible factor is the changing pattern of infant feeding, which might well affect the whole course of development, but the importance of this cannot easily be assessed.

In purely physical terms puberty makes a girl bigger and stronger, increases her physical endurance, and prepares for her future role in childbearing. Her ability to act quickly in emergencies and to move with speed and accuracy are also increased, so that there is an all-round improvement in skill. There are, however, three factors which may counteract these advantages.

Firstly, the eyesight often deteriorates at puberty because the growth spurt in the eye is more marked in the axial (back to front) diameter than it is in the vertical or transverse diameters. There is therefore a relative elongation of the eye which tends to cause short-sightedness.

Next menstruation is sometimes disadvantageous because it may be associated with headaches, abdominal pain or general malaise which reduce the girl's efficiency at her work. Many girls become anemic as a result of the repeated blood loss if their diet does not contain sufficient iron to counteract this. A mild chronic anemia of this type is a common cause of persistent tiredness and general lack of efficiency. A pubescent girl needs at least as much food as her mother, and her diet should be particularly rich in foods with a high content of protein and iron, such as meat, eggs, fish and liver.

The third factor which may act against the physical advantages of puberty is the psychological state of the girl at this time. This may prevent her from making full use of her potential skills, while long hours spent in the pursuit of pleasure may lead to lack of sleep unless common sense or parental control prevent this. Most adolescents need at least nine hours sleep each night in order to maintain their efficiency at a maximum.

Chapter 5

PERSONALITY

MARTHA HARRIS
Senior Child Psychotherapist
The Tavistock Clinic

The years from 5 to 12 were described by Freud as the "latency period", the part of a child's life when strong infantile sexual impulses are to some extent mastered, and so remain latent till reawakened in the bodily and emotional flowering of adolescence. But the repression of infantile sexuality and the control of primitive aggression is a gradual process, even a painful and reluctant one. And here the child is helped by the mother who wishes him to grow up, who is able to free him; by parents who expect, as his powers develop, increasingly responsible cooperation from him in governing his unruly impulses. He is stimulated by the very frustrations of his situation in the family to explore wider fields. [EDITORS' NOTE: *A more extensive discussion of this age, also from a psychoanalytic standpoint and with many case vignettes, will be found in Lidz (Chapters 6–8). Supplementary descriptions of personality development, extending beyond the customary realm of the psychoanalytic approach, will be found in Ferguson and in Mussen, Conger & Kagan. These books*

*add emphasis to such characteristics as the child's shift from dependence
on parents to peers, the devleopment of moral reasoning, achievement
and competence motivation, self-esteem, cooperation, and competition.*]

In the first years at school teachers act as parent substitutes, not
only to shelter and guide the child's inexperience of the world, but
also to protect him from the disruption of his own passions. They
make it easier for him, too, to identify with parents when they pro-
hibit sexuality, and so to accept the demands of the environment.
He makes common cause with others in the same predicament,
finds brothers and sisters outside the home, participates in little
groups where the children make and enforce their own laws derived from their interpretation of the laws of the adults who have
governed them hitherto. The child is sadly deprived if he is isolated
from his fellows, over-protected, confined to the prison of his infancy, to a love which grows more unrealizable and stifling.

For during these middle years he is learning, through participation in a social framework, knowledge, skills, values and confidence
in his power to create and to repair. He learns that satisfactions
may be enhanced by sharing them with members of his group, that
jealousies and defeats may be sweetened likewise.

The goal of sexual satisfaction, marriage and children, that in the
very young child's fantasy is realizable tomorrow if not today,
seems, if admitted at all by the latency child, very far away. During
the middle school years interest in children of the opposite sex is
often deprecated. But the basic need to come together in love with
others and to create together can be satisfied in work and in games.
During this period those games are popular which have a definite
structure, rules that take over parental sanctions, keep unruly egos
in check and serve as a protection for the weak. Through them the
child learns to try out various aspects of himself in different roles,
to express aggression constructively, to accept failure with a good
grace, to find allies to strengthen his position, to share success and
the responsibility of authority.

During these years friendships with other children assume increasing importance. A child may choose companions because of
mutual interests and prowess. His interests may be greatly influenced by the friends he makes. Apparently unlikely friendships

occur where each child expresses for the other attributes that he is unable to develop or to experience within his own personality: the athlete may join with the scholar, the successful pretty girl unaccustomed to, yet secretly fearing, defeat with the insignificant little mouse who vicariously enjoys success through her friend. Groups may form in which certain children fit into roles which express the needs of the others: the class dunce who conveniently carries the dullness of his companions, the naughty boy whose brushes with authority are regarded with gleeful disapproval by his more cowardly or conscientious friends. Children, as individuals and as groups, have their heroes and heroines who personify their aspirations. The sophistication and health of any little group can be judged fairly accurately by the personality of the leader.

It would be naive indeed to expect to be able to judge, or adequately to influence, the course of a child's development in the latency period by superficial external behavioristic criteria and recommendations. Should children paint more, or play more team games? Are "baddies and goodies" films and plays to be encouraged? Should groups of children make models of Everest, or should they compete in running races; should they hoard stamps or collect train numbers? Are the docile children better adjusted, or are the rebels in better shape? The demand for neatly typed categories and for a syllabus of life activities forgets that each child is one child, unique; and that all activities are necessary to all children. The answer is yes to everything. The advantages to society and to the individual are reciprocal. The social experience which the repression of sexual impulses makes possible, indeed enforces if the child is to grow at all, strengthens his power to cooperate and to discipline himself, in that it gives it a motive and reward; and this strengthening confidence relieves the inner tensions of the child. Yet it is tempting to overvalue the external evidence of adjustment and to underestimate the importance to society as well as to the individual child of the richness and harmony of the inner life.

With this in mind I propose to consider further the modes by which the latency child acquires his values, strives to achieve strength and integrity and to resolve the guilt which is part of being human.

The two great needs of the growing child, as of the adult, are to feel confident that he is alive, able to create, and that he is strong enough to take care of the people and things that he loves, both as they are in the outer world and as they exist in his mind. He needs to prove that his impulses to love and make are strong enough to repair some of the damage caused, in fact or fantasy, by his impulses to destroy and negate; for from the beginning of life, pain and frustration from within and without call forth such impulses. Frightened of his own aggression, the infant attributes it to whatever thwarts his will, thereby increasing its formidableness, from which he may retreat by annihilating his perception of it. Thus he creates fancied enemies, unreal projections: but in children, as in adult life, real dangers may creep up while we wrestle with ghosts.

An infant, if he is normally fortunate in his parents and in his own endowment, learns by repeated experiences of love and care how to love and care for others, and begins to distinguish between his own angry emotions and the hostile impingements of the outer world. With some recognition of dawning responsibility for his own destructiveness, he begins to realize that this is sometimes directed against the very person whom he loves and who both cherishes and frustrates him.

A little boy who at the age of 2 will often say spontaneously and affectionately "Sorry mummy", following outbursts of temper, may already, at the age of 7 months, be observed to check his impulse to bite the breast, after he has already done so, and felt his mother flinch. Thus guilt is born early in the infant, derived from the conflict between his love and hate directed toward the first person who has cared for him. It may spur the child on to reclaim the wastes of his hatred by love and reparation, or, when this is not possible, unconsciously to seek situations where he will be punished to appease a vengeful guilty conscience.

If his infantile fantasied omnipotent attacks on the mother have not been too violent and sustained, if they have been contained and humanized by maternal empathy and understanding, the very primitive retaliatory conscience created by them can be largely modified by experience. The bad figures of the fairy tales—typical personifications of this conscience—ferocious monsters, wicked step-mothers, dogs with saucer eyes, recede into the background of daily life and dreams. Unwarrantable retribution still plays its part in the sanctions of the playground:

> Tell tale tit,
> Your tongue shall be slit,
> And every dog about the place
> Shall have a little bit.

The 10 year old girl in tears because she has quarrelled with her best friend may actually feel abandoned by all her world and left naked to her enemies. But if she is able to find in herself a primary good experience of a secure and understanding person, she is better able to stand alone when need be and hold to her principles even if they happen to be unpopular with her friend or group. On the other hand, if she has wronged her friend, this secure internal core helps her to admit it and make amends.

Successes that are achieved too much on the basis of competition and at the expense of others build up a precarious self-confidence that is always liable to be assailed by the ghosts of the bodies over whom the triumph has been won, or to be destroyed by defeat. Such persecutory guilt is often at the base of sudden inexplicable failure. Thus James, an 11 year old boy, was referred for psychotherapy some months after the death of an elder brother, because of dramatic deterioration in hitherto excellent school work. When he related a nightmare about Hamlet's father's ghost it gradually emerged how his previous application and success had been strongly motivated by envious wishes to supplant his father (whom he consciously loved and admired) and his elder brother. The death of the latter had accentuated his unconscious guilt about the omnipotence of his destructive wishes, and inhibited the expression of his ambitions lest his father too should be swept out of the way in fact as well as fantasy. Failure in learning and in social adaptation may of course in some cases be invited by the overestimation of a child's capacity, by the school, or by unrealistically ambitious parents. In James' case, for instance, the hopes that the parents had entertained for the elder boy were then all invested in the younger and proved an additional and too heavy responsibility for him to carry.

On the other hand, parents who expect too little, who "baby" the child and do not encourage him to stretch toward his capacity, do not strengthen his faith in his ability to grow. Similarly abdication of parental authority, with idealization of the value of free expression of aggression, does not help children to evaluate realistically, and to take charge of their disruptive tendencies.

Solid achievement in skills and learning, in cooperative living with family, class and friends, prepares the child to face the stress of re-emerging sexuality at puberty, and to enjoy the unparalleled promise of adventure and fulfilment as an adult which then comes within his grasp. The building of this achievement in latency years depends upon the child's success in mastering within himself the omnipotent infant whose unrealistic ambitions would disrupt society. Yet, in the unconscious, nothing is finally relinquished: the infant is in us all, who sees the earth clad in the splendor of his desires and distorted by his terrors of the dark. Too severe a repudiation of the infantile part of himself leads in the latency child to division within the self. Such division may be typically exemplified in the impoverishment of imagination by an over-intensification of all the normal defenses against primitive anxieties, defenses which over-emphasize perception and control of external objects and stifle the spontaneous expression of emotion. The ostracized infantile part of the personality remains then undeveloped by the success of the growing child, and when reactivated at puberty may burst forth uncontrollably, or be perceived by the more efficient, rational part of the personality as such a threat that its suppression is redoubled and the adolescent is deprived of that reacquaintance with infantile emotion, the sources of anxiety and delight that are essential for the development of a rich maturity. If on the other hand infantile sexuality and aggression remain so much to the fore throughout the childhood years that they prevent any organized latency period, thereby interfering with organized work and play, the child is prevented from developing that experience in managing his environment and his impulses that is essential if he is to be able to weather adolescent storms.

Chapter 6

ABILITY

E. A. LUNZER

At 2 the child has learned to discriminate among a wide variety of different kinds of objects. He can anticipate the effects of his own actions in regard to these objects (the squeak of a toy, the texture and flexibility of cloth, the fall and roll of a ball, even the use of a light switch). He can also fend for himself in a large number of ways (feeding, finding his way about his own home and garden, and, to a more limited extent, dressing and recognizing his demand for elimination).

Superficially, by the age of 5 the child's abilities have extended quite considerably. He is now far more competent in looking after himself. For the most part he can dress and undress with little help; he can wash and go to the lavatory even though he may require supervision; where previously he knew only his own home, he now has some familiarity with its immediate neighborhood; he is thoroughly acquainted with the routines of home life: he knows what to expect and when to expect it, and will very likely be eager to help in doing things which he understands need to be (that is, are expected to be) done—for example, laying and clearing the table. He is also more skilled in the control of his own movements and more constructive in his use of material. He can solve simple jig-saw puzzles; he can cut paper into shapes; he may with some success fasten two pieces of wood to represent an airplane and play with this; he can draw a man with head, arms and legs as well as eyes, nose and mouth.

But these are mostly relatively minor extensions of the discriminations and competences that he had already achieved by the age of 2. There is a more fundamental gain. Throughout the period of early childhood (as opposed to infancy), the child is occupied in perfecting his *representation* of himself and his surroundings as experienced in the course of his actions: where the child of 18 months can discriminate and adapt in relation to a familiar environment, the 5 year old can reproduce the environment and the behavior in a variety of ways. Some we have already noted: drawing, construction, participation, and, one might add, most important of all, make-believe play. But side by side with these developments there is the highly significant elaboration of the most adaptable of all media of representation: language. The child of 2, if only average in development, expresses himself mainly in one or two word sentences; his spoken vocabulary has been estimated at something around 250 words. By contrast, the 5 year old may have a vocabulary of over 2,000 words. Even more significant is progress in mastering grammar and syntax.

By contrast with the total lack of experience and very limited behavioral discriminations available to the child at birth, the child of 5 may be considered to have accomplished a great part of those developmental tasks required for his integration into society. What are the developments that mark the next phase of development, the period from 5 to 11? Are these no more than a matter of a further extension in content and discriminative power along the lines of development already achieved in the preceding periods? Thus where the younger child can discriminate between shapes such as rectangles, squares and circles, the older child will have learned to discriminate between letters, and so will come to master the skill of reading (there is considerable evidence that the discrimination of letters can be achieved at much younger ages than 5 or 6). Where the younger child is familiar with a very few streets in his immediate neighborhood, the child of 10 or 11 will know something of the layout of the town in which he lives, and will appreciate its position relative to other places with which he has become acquainted either from his own experience or from his learning in school and at home. Certainly it is possible to catalogue the achievements of "preadolescents" in this way. Yet is there not, particularly in the area of intelligence and cognition, some more crucial departure peculiar to this phase of development?

The limitations in the communication of the 5 year old suggest that there is. Although he can represent his experience in language, he is unable to single out the relevant parameters of reality which would make his tale unambiguous to his listener. Piaget's investigations of the origins of reasoning led him to put forward the thesis that between the ages of 6 and 8 average children acquire certain ways of handling experience that are qualitatively different from earlier modes. Instead of merely reproducing and representing the experience as it was lived in the first instance, the child is able to make due allowance for the subjective element and so represent reality in objective terms. To take an example, a child of 5 or 6 is quite capable of finding his way to school and back and may be able to indicate this very crudely on a sand tray. But the accounts which he offers by way of describing his route are colored by his subjective experiences in following it. If he is in the habit of meeting a companion at some point on the journey, the meeting may become a landmark even though no permanent feature exists at the spot which would single it out as such. If he hurries on the way there and dawdles on the way back, he will strenuously deny that the route is equally long in either direction.

A major share in objectifying and systematizing experience lies in discovering concepts and measurements with which to categorize events and things. Such are the dimensions of space and time, and the categories of number, weight, temperature and so forth. To take a well-known example, children of 5 or 6 may be familiar with the language of number and yet generally lack an understanding of the *conservation* of number through changes in spatial arrangement.

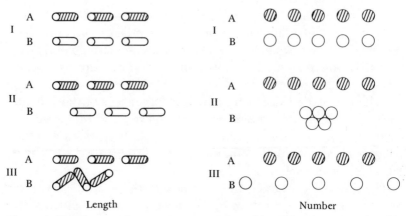

Length   Number

FIGURE 4. Situations used to assess conservation of length and number. In each situation children are asked to compare A with B after having established their equivalence in situation I and seen the change carried out on B that results in Situations II and III.

Having seen a row of eggs matched one for one against an equal row of egg-cups, they yet deny that there are as many eggs as egg-cups if the same eggs are then brought together in a cluster. Even though they realize that no eggs have been removed, they are over-impressed by the visual impression of length in the extended row of cups. The numerical equality which was made perceptible in the previous matching lacks permanence for them and is therefore outweighed by an illusory or fallible perceptual impression. By contrast, the 7 year old takes it for granted that if they were equal before they must remain equal. The numerical equality has been abstracted as something more significant, because more permanent and less subjective, than the visual impression.

In the same way a younger child cannot accept that if two rods are the same length when laid end to end, they remain the same length even if one of them is moved forward so that it projects beyond the other, and is therefore further away *from him*. The 8 year old thinks of length as an interval between two limits instead of regarding it, as a 5 year old does, as somehow vaguely connected with "far", "a long way", and so on, all of these being subjective ways of appreciating experience. One important reason that children acquire such ways of handling experience is that the models for such are all about them in the behavior of adults and older children. The mere copying of behavior is a necessary step in coming to understand its significance. [EDITORS' NOTE: *However, copying cannot explain how children acquire more mature modes of thinking; it may be necessary, but it clearly is not sufficient as an explanation.*]

Our next example is in the field of categorization itself. Suppose we give a child a set of pictures all of which are of rabbits: some are black and some are white, and within each group we have some squatting and others running. Even a 4 year old will probably be able to sort them into black versus white *or* squatting versus running. The 6 year old may well be able to divide them into black and white and *thereafter* into squatting and running. But it is only at 7 or 8 on average that children learn to carry out an immediate and systematic *cross classification*.

The new ways of systematizing are practically complete by the age of 9, and it is because the 9 and 10 year old classifies and systematizes his knowledge in much the same way that we do that he seems so much more adult both in the questions that he asks of us and in the ways in which he interprets and accepts the answers he receives. Limitations still persist where the accounts that he hears or reads of far outstrip his own experience. But the occasions when his conversation reveals the kind of confusion that leads us to describe it as "cute" are rare. The newly won power of systematization paves the way for that eagerness to learn which has always been recognized as one of the most prominent traits of the pre-adolescent.

Obviously there are considerable individual differences. Not only do some children develop more rapidly than others, but some are more often rewarded and accepted in their curiosity, while errors of knowledge or understanding may be less frequent and more readily tolerated. Where the vital "experience of success" is rare, the child may divert his curiosity from areas which he identifies with school work, though he may still be interested in collecting and categorizing information about trains, cars, footballers, pop singers and so on. In more extreme cases the apathy may be even more general, so that the terms curiosity and eagerness to learn seem hardly applicable. But the maladjusted child is not typical of the age group as a whole.

Finally, the reasoning of the pre-adolescent is still limited in important ways. When we pass from the facts themselves, and their systematization to their scientific explanation, he lacks the necessary power of abstraction. For such explanation involves setting up second-order relations between hypothetical *sets of data* and then testing the deductions that follow. Scientific and historical theories and the laws that compose them invariably go beyond the assignment of observable relations within a given set of events. They involve the construction and testing of hypothetical relationships. Second-order relations are not directly observable, nor can they be readily imagined. Hence the reasoning that they require is altogether more abstract. Its achievement belongs to the period of adolescence.

PART THREE

Adolescence: 12 to 18 years

*Part Three of our survey
of human development covers some crucial years.
Physical maturity is reached, internal conflict flares up
and complex logical thought becomes possible.*

Chapter 7

THE BODY

W. A. MARSHALL
Lecturer in Growth and Development
London University

The period of life between the 12th and 18th years might be described as the period of male ascendancy. At birth, boys tend to be slightly bigger in most dimensions than girls, but the difference is only of the order of 1 to 3 per cent in stature and the length of limbs. The earlier pubescence of girls makes them bigger and stronger than boys between the ages of about 10½ and 13, but when the boys have their growth spurt, they grow far more than the girls did and finish up some 10 per cent bigger.

The relative effect of the growth spurt on different parts of the body varies between the two sexes, and it is this variation which leads to many of the characteristic differences in body shape between men and women. The width of the hips increases as much in girls as in boys, but in all other dimensions there is a far greater increase in the male. The breadth of the shoulders and the breadth of the chest have particularly big increases in boys. The amount of bone and muscle in a boy's body increases greatly at adolescence, but fat is lost. In girls there is little increase in bone diameter, and fat is put on.

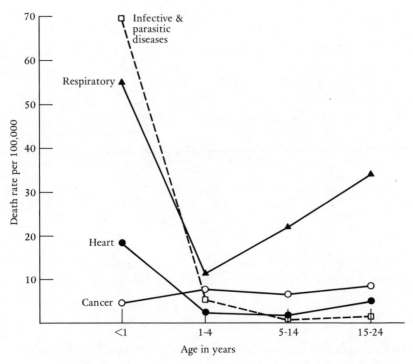

FIGURE 5. Death rates from major illnesses: birth to young adulthood. The plotted figures for each age group are the average numbers of deaths per year in each 100,000 persons of a given age in the total population. For example, in the four years included under age "1–4", the average number of deaths from respiratory disease was 11.4 per 100,000 children between the years of 1 and 4. The data are from the 1968 Mortality Statistics (Monthly Vital Statistics Report, U.S. Dept. of Health, Education and Welfare, 1971, vol. 19, No. 12. Comparable figures for ages 25 to 75 are given in the charts in Figures 9 and 10). Note the high incidence of death in the first year, but note also the historical trend of infant mortality shown in Figure 8.

While the changes in size and shape which are characteristic of puberty are taking place, there are also less obvious but equally important changes within the body. These physiological changes take place at the same time as the external ones, so that they occur early in those who have an early pubescence and late in those who have a late pubescence. Their overall effect is greatly to increase the strength of the individual and his capacity for physical exertion.

For example the rise in blood pressure which has been going on

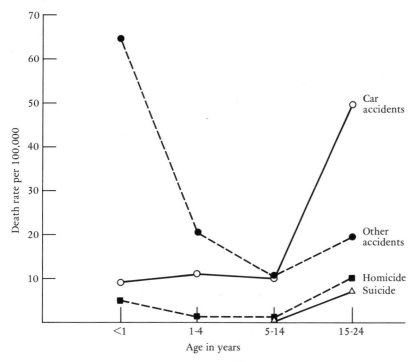

FIGURE 6. Death rates from major external causes: birth to young adulthood. The plotted figures are comparable to those in the illness chart. Note the frequency of homicide in the first year of life; these actual deaths do not fully reflect the incidence of serious injuries produced by enraged and insecure young parents, which constitutes "the battered child" phenomenon.

steadily throughout childhood accelerates sharply at puberty, so that final adult values are quickly reached. This rise is greater in boys than in girls, so that adult men have a slightly higher blood pressure than women. The heart rate becomes gradually slower throughout growth. In boys the number of red cells in the blood rises markedly at the time of puberty, and the amount of hemoglobin, the substance which carries oxygen, is also increased. The total volume of blood in the body also increases to a greater extent in boys than in girls.

In addition, the normal rate of breathing decreases throughout childhood and on through puberty in both sexes; but the maximum amount of air which can be breathed in a given time, or at a single breath, increases markedly in adolescent boys while there is little, if any, increase in girls. Moreover, the amount of air which must be taken into the lungs in order to pass a given amount of oxygen to the blood becomes less in boys than in girls. There is a further mechanism whereby, during severe exercise, the muscles can function even with an inadequate supply of oxygen by producing lactic acid and incurring what is known as an "oxygen debt". This mechanism improves in efficiency at puberty and continues to improve at least until the age of 19 years. As a result of all these changes more oxygen can be made available to exercising muscle while the muscles themselves become capable of greater activity even beyond the limits of their increased oxygen supply. The total capacity for physical work is thus increased enormously in boys and to a lesser extent in girls.

The strength of the muscles increases to an even greater extent than their increasing size would suggest. Both the strength of arm thrust and the strength of arm pull become much greater in boys as their shoulder, back and chest muscles grow. These changes are less marked in girls. The strength of hand grip is greater in boys even before puberty because boys' forearms are bigger from the time of birth onwards. Both boys and girls show a marked increase at puberty in the distance which they can put a 12 lb shot, and boys also show a marked improvement in their running ability. There is good evidence that greater gains in strength occur in the spring than in the winter. A similar seasonal effect on growth in height can be seen at all ages.

It is said that menarche marks approximately the end of the increase of strength in girls, and it is true that girls' performances in many athletic events seem to deteriorate after the age of 14 or 15. This may simply be because girls have less motivation to do well at this type of task as they grow up.

An important aspect of the growth spurt in strength is that it may not occur for some time after the spurt in height. Growth in the size of the muscles is, however, only delayed by a very short time in relation to the height spurt, so that the muscles grow first in size and only later in strength, and there may be a gap of a year or more between the time when a boy reaches almost adult stature and has the muscular appearance of a man, and the time when he has in fact attained something approaching adult strength. This has given rise to the popular notion of a boy outgrowing his strength. There is in fact no time during adolescence when strength is not increasing, and it is certainly not true that the changes accompanying adolescence have any weakening effect.

The greatest improvement in boys' muscular coordination occurs at the same time as strength increases most rapidly and some time after the greatest growth in size has already taken place. This time lag has given rise to another popular misconception, that adolescents become less skilled, particularly in balance, while they are growing rapidly. There is no evidence to support this view, and a more reasonable explanation of the adolescent's apparent clumsiness is that for a short period of time his skill is not as close to its maximum as his size, although it never becomes less.

The time which a boy takes to react to a sudden stimulus decreases markedly between the ages of 14 and 18. This change is of obvious value in sports and in types of work where quick reactions are necessary.

One of the most important aspects of male pubescence is the variability in the age at which it may occur. As with girls, there is a trend towards earlier maturation. Some 14-year-old boys have reached sexual maturity and are virtually adult in size, strength, skill and outlook, while others of the same age are, for practical purposes, small boys. There is a tendency for educational and other administrators to legislate for all boys of the same age as if they were physical and social equals while, in fact, a post pubescent boy of 13 will be more at home with a group of older post pubescent boys than will a 15 year old who is just entering puberty. The boy whose pubescence is late frequently suffers serious emotional disturbance because his associates of the same age are not only sexually mature but are far bigger and stronger than he is. When this boy eventually has his growth spurt, he may well become a bigger and more manly individual than any of those whom he may in earlier years have envied.

By the age of 18 most girls have completed their growth and passed the stage at which their physical skills are greatest. Boys on the other hand are improving in all their physical attributes up to this age and further improvements are yet to come, although in size, strength and skill they have already surpassed all but the most exceptional girls.

Chapter 8

PERSONALITY

DEREK MILLER
The Adolescent Unit,
The Tavistock Clinic

Despite the chronological vagueness of the adolescent age period, it is nevertheless a specific period in human development in most cultures. It is characterized by increased conflict with oneself and the outside world and a high growth potential, physically, intellectually and emotionally. The dilemma as to what is meant by adolescence has to an extent been resolved by young people who have created their own social norms and see themselves as adolescent while they are in their teens.

The first obvious attempt to differentiate between self and non-self, "me" and "them", occurs when a child at the age of 2 begins to defy parental authority and say "No". During adolescence the individual further differentiates himself from others. Relationships outside the family become intense, and, as part of the process of being individuals, the adolescent group, in particular boys, tends to separate out "we" and "they". Whether "they" are perceived as hostile depends partly on the attitudes of the outside world, partly on the adolescent's psychological maturity. [EDITORS' NOTE: *The*

*most influential personality theory concerning adolescence is that of
Erikson (1968). He feels the main task of adolescence is establishing
identity. Various manifestations of the search for identity include seeking
behavioral and emotional autonomy, alienation from adults and especially from parents, strong involvement with peer groups, concern with
and advocacy of different philosophies of life, involvement in politics,
use of drugs, and so forth. Vocational choice is a stronger influence on
identity for boys than for girls.*]

Early adolescence, 11 to 15 in girls, 12 to 16 in boys, corresponds
with puberty. Because of the rapid acceleration of growth, especially
of arms and legs, and the size and shape of hands, feet and face, individuals feel their bodies as disharmonious and are no longer at ease
with themselves. They are likely to become negativistic, questioning
and defiant.

This behavior is a necessary testing of the limits of control and
freedom, but it also represents a demand for both. This is the age of
secrecy from adults, particularly parents, a part of a technique of
emotional separation which allows for increasing independence. To
adults the early adolescent may at times appear to be egoistic, vain,
proud and aggressive; at others helpless and dependent. On the one
hand he seems capable of loyalty, self-sacrifice and devotion; on the
other of utter selfishness. It is also an age of movement, and physical
activity is used both as a tension-relieving device and as a way of
communicating with others.

For both sexes in early adolescence formal and informal group
formation is common. Transient gang formation occurs particularly
with boys, although its extent varies between social classes and from
culture to culture. The individual boy is often quite exhibitionistic
with his peers and talks freely with them of highly intimate problems.

Girls, on the other hand, become increasingly modest and yet
increasingly aware of the opposite sex. Groupings of girls are more
apparent than real; unless they are forced to live in an artificial uni-
sexual environment, their relationships with each other are only
transient, if often intense.

In late adolescence, 15 to 19 in girls, 16 to 20 in boys, with its
increasing harmony of bodily features, healthy adolescents are able
increasingly to accept and come to terms with themselves and the

demands of reality, and in turn they can appropriately modify the demands they make on society. Individual talents and interests flower. This is the Indian summer of youth, and after its passing one has to begin to face the awareness of mortality.

In both early and late adolescence intense self-contradiction is often experienced. The adolescent loves and hates, communicates freely, and yet, when feeling misunderstood, as abruptly withdraws. The individual is at once submissive and rebellious, ascetic and self-indulgent, selfish and idealistic. Full of energy at one moment, and the next feeling overwhelmingly lazy, the adolescent varies between optimism and a preoccupation with the drab desert of the world. He is often too absorbed with the discrepancy between how he feels himself to be and how others see him. Various roles in both fantasy and reality are tried on, rather as fashionable attire changes. Much of this alternation can be seen as an attempt to establish a secure identity. [EDITORS' NOTE: *Every generation seems to have its favorite symptoms of maladjustment. In the 19th Century and up through World War I, hysterical conversion symptoms were in style. Between the wars, anxiety neuroses became wide-spread, especially among the affluent who could afford treatment. With the growing articulateness of the late adolescent, and the increasing availability of mental health facilities for children after World War II, the* identity crisis *appeared on the scene. It is a real phenomenon—but perhaps a little more "real" since it was labelled. For a sensitive and clear discussion, see Erickson, 1968.*]

The way a child is treated by parents and its identification with their perceived qualities, assists the process by which the infant becomes a "masculine boy" or a "feminine girl". Both these factors apply again with renewed intensity in the development of the sexual identification of the adolescent. Because of the inner turmoil of the period, throughout adolescence it is necessary to test the strength of, and consolidate, this identification. By the time late adolescence supervenes, the boy should be capable of mature physical relationships.

The first testing of oneself as a sexual male normally occurs, in our society, by the almost universal process of masturbation with heterosexual fantasies. At first boys establish their feelings of masculinity in relationship to members of the same sex. This is done by comparing physical, sexual and intellectual prowess with one's age mates. A sexual love of one's own sex, which tends to be a male prerogative, may in relatively closed masculine societies become overtly sexual with episodes of mutual sexual exploration which do not necessarily lead to an ultimate homosexual inclination. [EDITORS' NOTE: *Figures on relative frequency of male and female homosexuality are notoriously difficult to interpret. The openness of the male in his reports contrasts with the seemingly greater caution of the female. The delicate nuances of exploration, affectionate dependency, "crushes," and romantic involvements are simply lost in the survey studies that report "frequencies" of any kind of sexual behavior, including homosexual.*]

In our society, a boy's first relationship with a girl is likely to be transient and highly experimental. It is as if the girl is a medal which a boy wears to prove his masculinity to his peers. Although a boy usually realizes how hurtful this attitude is toward a girl, he is often all too willing to derogate her by discussing his real and fantasied promiscuity. This need to derogate women would appear to allow a boy to revenge himself unconsciously on a girl for her feminine productivity, with which he cannot compete. [EDITORS' NOTE: *The boy's derogation has other sources, too. It can serve as an outlet for the hostility caused by fear of the girl as a sex object, a fear created by early family experiences that made sexual advances forbidden behavior. Furthermore, girls at a given age are more mature than boys. This, coupled with their greater conformity to propriety and conservative social norms, makes them targets for complaint from the insecure and rebellious young male.*]

In later adolescence the girl friend may still be used by a boy to show his male friends his potency, but this should be becoming a tender, private, meaningful relationship. Young men do not normally appear to be highly promiscuous; when sexual relationships occur, they are felt to be intense and last for a considerable time, although they may be quite exhibitionistic.

The menarche provides for girls a dramatic proof of their femininity, and they appear to establish this from the outset largely in relationship to boys, although they may compare themselves physically with each other, particularly as regards breast development. Masturbation in girls would not appear to be as necessary for normal development as in boys.

Apart from other factors, such as envy of masculine status, a girl, who tries out her budding femininity in a one-to-one relationship with a boy, is far more likely to be emotionally hurt than he, because she is likely to "fall in love" and fantasy permanence to the relationship. [EDITORS' NOTE: *For a girl much of her future identity is tied up with her husband—thus involvement in stable heterosexual relations may be part of the search for identity. For males, however, a "steady girl friend" may impede that trying on of a multitude of roles which is important for the establishing of identity.*] Partially because of the different rates of psychological maturation of the sexes, partially because of social pressures, the boy is less likely to want this permanence and most unlikely to want marriage. Thus all too often the girl's attempt to use her femininity in a constructive way, in an interpersonal relationship, is thwarted, and she is left not only feeling unloved but also unlovely.

It is probably better in our society for the girl in early adolescence, frustrated in her attempts to establish close relationship with boys by her parents' refusal to give her the necessary freedom, to be angry with them, than for her to be given too much freedom and then be hurt.

In general terms adolescence begins with the onset of the wish to be emotionally independent and sexually active; it ends with the completion of sexual identification, a choice of profession and a place for oneself in society.

The adolescent must be looked at as an individual, but he or she is also a member of a family and of society at large. The adolescent boy feels increasingly ready to abandon childhood security. He wishes for independence long before he is able to handle the complexities of modern living. These, plus his inner uncertainty, may from time to time force a boy to wish to abandon his desire for independent judgment and action. On such occasions, to maintain his integrity, he angrily tends to feel that his motives are misunderstood and unreasonable demands are being made upon him. On the other hand, all too often his demands are perceived as intolerably unrealistic by parents or society. One way in which parents deal with their anxiety and anger about this is to withdraw emotionally; they thus become unable to perceive in a constructive manner how much responsibility the adolescent is able to handle. This relative rejection is more likely because the adolescent often represents to the parents an unconscious sexual or aggressive threat.

In girls the balance between dependence and independence is weighed more heavily toward the former. They tend to confide more in their mothers than boys with either parent. They establish a separate identity from their mothers by being alternately highly aggressive towards them, and then by literally and metaphorically borrowing their mother's clothing.

Girls have a need to be looked after. [EDITORS' NOTE: *This repre-sents a common stereotype about females. Boys, too, need to be looked after. Dependency and autonomy develop in a complex and delicate balance in every human being. However, it appears that girls are more responsive to their parents' opinions, boys to their peers'.*] Since society makes fewer economic demands on a girl, it is possible for her to stay at home and help with the house. If psychological illness comes as a psycho-social withdrawal, it is more socially acceptable than for boys. Thus if a girl does present herself to a doctor with a psycholog-ical illness, or to the courts as delinquent, she is probably more dis-turbed than the equivalent boy.

Parents, too, have their difficulties. The growing independent needs of an adolescent son or daughter represent to a mother a threat of potential unemployment from her vocation of mothering. Feeling devalued by herself, her family and society, mothers then often act to keep the adolescent dependent. In addition, some fathers in their social prime as their children become adolescent may have the par-ticular problem of envying their sons' greater sexual freedom than the father enjoyed as an adolescent. They are also uncomfortably aware of the sexuality of their daughters. It is not unusual for the onset of late adolescence in a child, with the individual's drive for freedom, to unveil a marital conflict that has been hidden by the joint parental task of husband and wife which has now been rela-tively lost.

Society may be permissive towards adolescence: the provocative behavior of youth is sometimes tolerated. However, extreme incon-sistences pervade society's attitude. Although standards are in a con-stant state of flux, society at large expects the adolescent to complete sexual identification without sexual experience, make a choice of profession often with minimal immediate economic and social rewards, and to take a place in society as a responsible citizen and yet not be able to influence its course in any direct manner.

The adolescent's difficulties are, then, enhanced by the contradictory and complex demands and perceptions of society at large which do not necessarily fit with the adolescent's concept of himself. In Western Society the adolescent seems to some extent to represent the repository of the projections of the cultural environment. In a culture which tends to be hypermoralistic and somewhat hypocritical about its own use of aggression, all adolescents are loosely considered to be licentious and delinquent. Yet when adolescents do behave in an aggressive or hypersexual manner, adults appear to gain vicarious satisfaction from this. Riots by gangs of youths on beaches are watched in fascinated horror by adult groups who seem almost unwittingly to obstruct the efforts of police forces to control them.

There are, however, advantages as well as disadvantages in the confused attitudes of society at large. Well institutionalized patterns for the adolescent relieve anxiety but do not allow for the ultimate production of a flexible personality.

The end of adolescence comes with the completion of certain vital social tasks. The adolescent, if he lives in a mobile society, has to cope with separation from parents, siblings and childhood friends. Anyway he must become psychologically autonomous. This autonomy, whether or not it is associated with physical separation from the original family group, should carry with it the capacity to make decisions, to regulate one's own behavior and to assume responsibility for oneself. The parents now are there to be loved but not depended upon. Finally, the adolescent has to deal with new intellectual and economic challenges. The effectiveness with which these tasks are accomplished and the emotional cost of completing them is a measure of successful growth through adolescence. [EDITORS' NOTE: *For a more extensive discussion of many of the points in this section, see Lidz, Chapter 10.*]

Chapter 9

ABILITY

KENNETH LOVELL
Lecturer in Educational Psychology,
Leeds University

By adolescence the individual has had a dozen years or more of interaction with his environment, and these years are of importance in determining his abilities displayed at school or work.

It has long been known that differences in the general quality of the central nervous system seem likely to be a major cause of the variation in intellectual abilities between individuals, that is, in their capacity for coordinating complex actions carried out in the mind. But it is now known that other influences are also important. Children who receive parental encouragement, or experience good teaching and a stimulating environment, or children who are emotionally stable, or whose thoughts are not too greatly disturbed by fantasy, are all likely to develop greater abilities than would otherwise be the case, since they tend to build up over the years a mental organization that is richer and more flexible. Moreover, emotional stability, introversion and persistence (which is linked with introversion), all influence, even before adolescence, the degree to which young people can steadfastly apply their abilities to school and other work, thereby affecting school attainment and work performance.

To about 12 years of age a child's thoughts are closely tied to concrete situations in his immediate experience. But from 12 onwards, new and important thinking skills begin to emerge. Due to his continuing interaction with the social *milieu* and the maturation of the central nervous system, the adolescent can increasingly elaborate more complex expectancies when faced with certain kinds of data. His logical thought now extends to statements of propositions relating to objects and their properties. To illustrate this point suppose that a pupil is presented with a length of string suspended from a hook, and that one of several weights can be attached to the lower end. The subject is asked to establish what determines the period of oscillation of this simple pendulum. He can change the attached weight, vary the length of the string, alter the height from which the "bob" is released and the impetus, if any, he imparts to it initially. The adolescent can reason that *if* some particular variable (e.g. length of string) affects the time of swing, then the effect will appear *if* he holds the other variables constant and varies only the one he is considering. On the other hand, if he decides on, say, weight as the crucial influence, and he carried out a corresponding procedure and found no effect on the time of swing, then he must rule out weight alone as a factor.

In essence the pupil has to consider the *merely* possible, work out the consequences if the hypothesis is true, and then verify or confirm the consequences. These new skills become available at what Piaget called the stage of *formal thought*. They become increasingly available to the secondary school pupil in mathematics, science, history, literature, etc. But, for reasons not well understood, formal thought does not develop in all areas or in all situations simultaneously.

The adolescent can now build a new kind of concept, for he is no longer confined to those that are constructed out of immediate reality. He can increasingly coordinate relationships between concepts already constructed and build new concepts of a higher level of abstraction. Thus the concept of *proportion* becomes available, for an analogy of the form 3:4 as 15:20 involves a relationship between the first two terms (3, 4), another between the second pair (15, 20), and the establishment of the identity relationship between these two relationships. The logical structure of such a system is exactly parallel to that of a statement of proportionality. Likewise the adolescent can combine the concepts of *mass* and *temperature* and elaborate the concept of *heat* (mass x temperature). Whereas mass and temperature are mental constructs derived directly from the environment, their product is not.

Unfortunately there are many important questions relating to the growth of formal thought that cannot yet be answered. For example, what percentage of adolescents reach this stage of thinking? Can the onset of such thought be speeded up by suitable education? Is the interaction with the social *milieu*, or the zeitgeist, all important? What part does language play? Only future research can answer these questions. If, however, the thinking skills demanded of the adolescent are too far ahead of those available to him, he will assimilate, with distortion, what he is taught, and there will be no transfer to similar situations. But it does seem likely that one of the reasons that adolescents are argumentative and in verbal rebellion against adult standards is that for the first time they can reflect on their own thoughts and feelings, hypothesize, and see that the way in which adults run the world is one of a number of possible ways.

If to a group of, say, 14 year olds of varying scholastic attainments a series of tasks is given involving words and the meaning of words, mechanical and problem arithmetic, the imaginative manipulation of shapes, and mechanical knowledge, the variation in the performance among the pupils can be accounted for by positing one main and two group abilities.

The general ability, called *g* by Spearman, contributes something to all the tests. It is a matter of grasping relationships and is most strongly in evidence in the more complex intellectual tasks like reasoning or abstraction. One group ability is a verbal-numerical-educational or v:ed ability; the other the practical-mechanical-spatial or k:m ability.

The former indicates the ability to understand both written and spoken words and to benefit from a verbal type of education. The latter divides into: (a) spatial ability or the capacity to perceive and retain mentally an impression of the form of a shape or pattern as a whole and (b) mechanical ability which depends on knowledge and experience of mechanical apparatus and operations. Physical abilities like speed of running, and abilities involved in manual dexterities, e.g. speed of screwing nuts on bolts, correlate with the k:m ability to some extent, but they are largely specific to the tasks involved.

Both group abilities depend upon inborn potential and cultural opportunities and are linked to temperament. The k:m ability is in evidence by 11 years of age, but in our society is less well developed in girls than in boys. This may be partly due to the different kinds of activities in which the sexes engage from the early years. However, g would account for some 40 per cent, and the two group abilities for some 15-20 per cent, of the variability in the performance of given tasks.

The longer the training required for a particular job and the more complex the activities involved in it, the higher the level of abilities generally needed. Thus an adolescent wanting to enter a profession must obtain fairly high scores on the general and verbal-educational abilities. With more modest scores, but still above average, he is likely to be suitable for a variety of occupations ranging from salesman to toolmaker; while if his scores are average or a little below he may well be successful as a skilled craftsman such as electrician or plumber. Semi-skilled and unskilled workers score lower. Within any occupation, however, there is a great range of ability, so that some toolmakers will score higher than some accountants.

Spatial-mechanical ability is of more limited value in predicting scholastic performance, and its chief value lies in predicting competence in employment. For example, spatial-mechanical ability contributes (together with general ability) to performance in watch repairing; also to the competence of architects, civil and mechanical engineers, and draftsmen. On the other hand the ability contributes little to one's performance as a lawyer, clerk, salesman or poultry farmer.

Between 15 and 18 there are differential changes in abilities. Vernon adduced strong evidence that general ability grows only as long as educational or other stimulation occurs. While intelligence test scores continue to rise to 25 years of age or more in students, maximum scores are reached at 15 by those who have no further education. Vocabulary size increases beyond 18, although ability to do arithmetic remains stationary for a few years after 15 or declines somewhat, unless stimulated by further schooling or work. The k:m ability increases up to the late teens.

This conceptual framework for the structure of abilities is widely accepted by British psychologists. But Eysenck and White have indicated that recent work among 15-16 year olds suggests that in emotionally labile adolescents, abilities are less clearly structured. Greater emotional stability and ability, respectively, may go with greater degrees of organization of ability and stability. Further, it must be stressed that the g, v:ed and k:m abilities are not identical with the degree and speed of learning new skills, although there is a positive correlation with these abilities in complex learning tasks. Indeed, there is little evidence that there is a general learning ability common to a wide variety of tasks—psychomotor, mechanical, verbal and non-verbal, rote and meaningful.

Those giving educational and vocational guidance to adolescents rightly attempt to assess their intellectual abilities and educational attainments. After this, their success is likely to depend mainly on how well they can assess the adolescent's relevant experience, personality traits, interests and general motivation, and then attempt to assess his specific attitudes to the type of education or job under consideration.

PART FOUR

Young Adult: 18 to 30 years

*The fourth part of our survey of human development
describes how we reach our peak physically and in terms of aptitudes.
Yet we often find it hard to face the emotional pressures
of marriage, parenthood and work.*

Chapter 10

THE BODY

W. A. MARSHALL
Lecturer in Growth and Development,
London University

The physical state of the human individual reaches its highest level between the ages of 18 and 30. Growth in stature is completed and men attain their highest skill at those tasks which involve speed and agility, while in women the ability to bear and rear children is greatest at this age. Growth of the limbs in most young men and women is completed by the time they are 18, but the vertebral column continues to grow slightly. This leads to a very slight increase in stature of the order of one fifth of an inch between the ages of 20 to 30. There is also a very slight increase in the measurement of the head and face.

In his recent book, *The Physique of the Olympic Athlete*, Dr. J. M. Tanner describes the physical characteristics of 137 athletes of Olympic standard. Only 21 of these were over 30 years of age, and only one was under 18. All those who competed in events demanding extremes of speed or agility, such as short distance running, jumping or hurdling were in the under 30 age group.

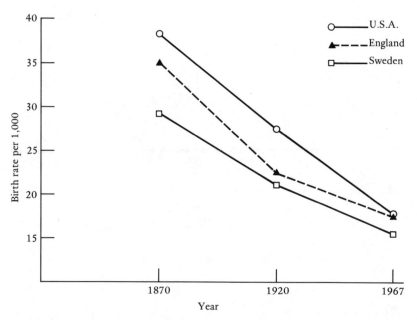

FIGURE 7. Birth rate: the number of births per 1,000 population. As infant mortality decreased and as education and urbanization increased, the birth rate fell precipitously in all three countries.

Thus exceptional men are capable of the highest standards of speed and agility at this age, but there is evidence that more ordinary men, too, are capable of their own highest individual performances at this time. The strength of grip increases up to the age of about 30, and the strength of muscles involved in other activities increases also. The extent to which the strength of muscles can be increased by training is still going up during this period of life in men, but not in women. The ability of men to adapt physiologically to violent and prolonged exercise by incurring an oxygen debt, as discussed in the previous chapter, is also still increasing. In athletes there may be some slight enlargement of the heart in adaptation to years of training. This is due to an increase in the amount of cardiac muscle and leads to greater functional efficiency. There is no ground for the belief that excessive enlargement and strain of the heart results from too much exercise in normal individuals.

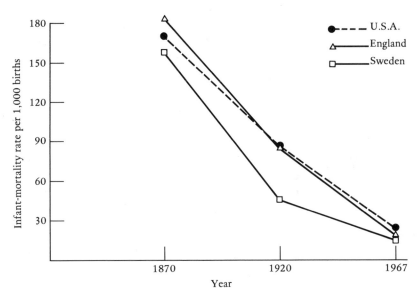

FIGURE 8. Infant mortality: the number of deaths during the first year per 1,000 live births. Even the last half century has seen marked improvement for all three countries, but Sweden maintains a comfortable lead.

In those who are not subjected to athletic training, most physiological functions change little at this stage of life. The blood pressure remains at about its adolescent value, being very slightly higher in men than women, while the heart rate is about 10 per cent greater in women than in men. This may be simply due to the fact that the body temperature is about half a degree Fahrenheit higher in women than in men.

It is usually after the age of 18 that adult physique becomes finally established in men. Each person's physique may be regarded as being made up of three components known as "Endomorphy", "Mesomorphy" and "Ectomorphy". A person who has a high degree of endomorphy, and little ectomorphy and mesomorphy, approaches spherical in shape and has a large abdomen of greater diameter than his chest. His internal organs are relatively large for his general body size. He is usually very fat, but this is not essential to his physique: if starved he will still be an endomorph and will not change into someone whose physique is high in either ectomorphy or mesomorphy.

Mesomorphy represents the proportion of bone and muscle in the body, and the classical Hercules is typical of the individual in whose physique this component predominates. A high degree of ectomorphy produces the slender individual with little fat or muscle but a large area of skin and a large nervous system in proportion to the size of his body as a whole. Persons representing the extreme in any one of these components are rare, and the population cannot be divided into groups of endomorphs, ectomorphs or mesomorphs. All three components are present in varying degrees in each individual, and their various combinations form a continuous spectrum throughout the population.

It is a common observation that different types of temperament tend to be associated with different body builds, and the final choice of one's career is also to some extent influenced by one's physique as it reflects a temperamental inclination to follow one sort of life rather than another. For example, one would not choose to become an instructor of physical education unless one had some athletic ability and were good at games oneself. One might expect to find similar qualities of physique in those who choose to enter the armed forces. On the other hand, there seems to be some tendency for those of more slender build to be interested in the less practical and more academic pursuits. In one study it was shown that those on the research side of a factory at all age levels were more linear than those on production. Both long distance transport drivers and airline pilots have been shown to be more muscular than the general population. These last two occupations might well reflect the same basic aptitudes and interests at different levels of intelligence and education.

Many men in their 20s give up their former sports and athletic pursuits, although they have sedentary jobs. They no longer need the high calorie content of the diet to which they have become accustomed, but the eating habits developed during adolescence are often continued and obesity results. This, in varying degrees, is a common phenomenon in the less athletic members of this age group, who may pay for their indiscretions many years later in terms of early disability or death, from high blood pressure or the degenerative diseases. In general the food requirements of women at this age tend to be lower than those of men, but this does not necessarily apply in those households where the man's work is sedentary and the woman does all her own housework. Women need more iron in their diet than do men, in order to make good the loss of blood which results from menstruation. Mild degrees of anemia resulting from iron deficiency are common.

In the special circumstances of pregnancy and lactation a woman's diet must be greatly increased in both quantity and quality. The diet of a pregnant woman should provide at least 2,500 calories and 85 grams of protein. This is comparable with the dietary requirements of a man who leads a fairly sedentary life. The pregnant woman's intake of calcium (e.g. in milk) and iron should be higher than that of a man. During lactation an even higher intake of both energy foods and protein is necessary, the calorie requirement being about 3,000, as in the case of a moderately active man, and something of the order of 100 grams of protein is required, as compared with the average man's requirement of 70 grams. If a pregnant or lactating woman's diet is inadequate, her own health is likely to suffer before that of her baby, but her efficiency as a mother may be reduced to such an extent that the child's health is also affected.

It is the common experience of the doctors and midwives that the delivery of a first baby in a woman over 30 is likely to be more diffi-cult than it is in a younger woman. In older women the tissues are less elastic and it is less easy for the head of a child to make its way through the birth canal without sustaining damage to itself. The ease with which subsequent babies are born is less influenced by the age of the mother.

Only very slight changes can be detected in the brain and sensory organs of young adults, and the significance of these changes is ob-scure. The weight of the brain appears to decline slowly at the rate of about one gram a year from the 20th year of life onwards. The average weight of a man's brain at this period of life is slightly greater than that of a woman's, but the size of the brain is no indication of the intelligence or wisdom of the individual. The adult pattern of EEG activity appears to be established in the late teens and remains fairly constant until old age. Different individual patterns may be related to personality types, but these relationships are not well established. Electroencephalography is anyway only a very gross method of study, since it records a very small sample of synchronous activity from the brain surface. Most of the more complicated activities of the brain, underlying conscious sensation, thought and behavior cannot be closely related to changes in the EEG pattern.

The sense organs show little change in young adult life. There is a slight difference in hearing ability between the two sexes in that men are less able than women to detect high tones. It is not certain when this difference becomes established, but it is probably before adolescence. The lens of the eye loses some of its elasticity and becomes less able, therefore, to change shape and focus on near objects. This is a continuation of a hardening process which probably begins at about the age of 10 and is an example of aging beginning in early life. By the age of 30, however, the changes are seldom sufficient to produce a significant effect on the function of the eyes. Any very slight loss of functional efficiency in the sensory mechanism of the young adult is more than compensated for by the fact that he has been trained to make fuller and more profitable use of his senses than he did as a child.

By the age of 30 the typical young adult is married, has produced at least the beginning of a family, has passed the peak of both ability and inclination for violent physical exercise and is ready to enter the settled phase of family life.

Chapter 11

PERSONALITY

HARRY GUNTRIP
Department of Psychiatry,
Leeds University

No single statement about any age is true of everybody. There is
no monotonous sameness embracing all human beings. If by the
characteristics of 18-30 we mean those that will be shown by individuals who have matured normally through their first 18 years,
there will still be infinite variety; and we must add that there are
always many individuals who are younger than their years, and
others who seem older. With these reservations, we must characterize 18-30 as the first phase of adulthood. Practically and emotionally the major problem is to establish oneself in a position of one's
own, which carries with it economic and domestic independence of
parents. If relations with parents are good, the earlier dependence is
gradually being replaced all through adolescence by "friendship on
a footing of human equality", but this can only be completed in the
young adult stage. If it is achieved in a mature and healthy way,

it does not involve any drastic breakaway from the old home, quarrels with or repudiation of parents, or a "know all" attitude of regarding them as old fogies. But parents need to be mature too and recognize that the young can grow up to real knowledge and wisdom.

Some of the most difficult problems of these years may be forced on young adults by immature and anxious parents who still think of them as "the children" and cling to their supposed right to go on telling them what they ought to do. The happiest and mentally healthiest state is that in which the older folk feel free to express an opinion in general discussions but do not try to press their advice; and the young adults show plenty of initiative and originality in living in their own age group but are not afraid to talk things over and occasionally seek advice from their older folk. Complete cleavages between different age levels rest on mutual distrust, insecurity and defensive attitudes which are unhappy signs of disturbed personalities. The basic inner sense of security as a personality, which is so important to everyone, is closely related to smooth continuity of development.

One environmental factor affecting this today is the extreme rapidity of change in our material circumstances. It is easy to become out of date so quickly now, that a graduate in the late 20s said to me, "The undergrads of today simply speak a different language from those of my time." The young adults of 18-30, building up their new homes and independent careers and way of life, are in the thick of this pressure of rapid and revolutionary changes affecting every aspect of living. They may easily fall out of sympathy with older people who have their different established ways of living and who feel no need to make more than minimal changes in them; and the older people in turn may fail to appreciate and sympathize with, or feel the stimulus experienced by, younger adults who are living in their own faster moving world. Thus, lack of mental contact between younger and older adults can grow to the detriment of both. [EDITORS' NOTE: *Not all changes are progressive. Some of today's grandparents, who were accustomed to trains, can recall the success of a short airplane ride as a birthday present for their own children in the '30s and '40s. Now they can enthrall their grandchildren with a* train *ride!*]

One of the subtle psychological problems of young adulthood is that emotional ties to parents persist in the unconscious long after economic and domestic independence have been achieved. If they are too completely denied recognition, they may well force themselves into expression in disguised and neurotic ways. This, in fact, remains true for human beings to the very end of life. The unconscious persistence of the original parent child patterns of relationship plays a very large part in shaping all kinds of human relations at all ages, but this is never more important than in young adulthood, when the most momentous and significant relationships are entered into—in marriage, parenthood and in some cases professional and business commitments.

Thus marriage choices are often, perhaps always, due to a mixture of realistic objective attraction to someone who is physically, temperamentally, intellectually and socially a genuine partner, and unconscious emotional attractions and repulsions deriving from the relationships of childhood. In addition to objectively realistic factors, a marriage choice may be influenced by attraction to a parental type, or by repulsion from the parental type (i.e. attraction to the opposite type), or by a search for something in personal relationship which parents were not able to give, or by a need to turn the tables on a parent by carrying on old struggles with a substitute person (which not seldom makes a bad marriage impossible either to break or mend).

These types of problems emerge all over again when young adults become parents in their own right. Today, when an increasing amount of psychological "know how" is becoming available to young parents, and they seek to apply their intelligently acquired views on how to treat children to their parental responsibilities, conflict and stress may result. They can find themselves at times of emotional tension thinking one way and behaving another. Thus a young woman whose mother says she beat her daughter's temper out of her, and who thinks of herself as a tolerant and good-natured person, becomes in turn a mother. She may then be assailed by acute anxiety attacks every time her baby cries and discover to her horror that it is because she felt a powerful urge to beat her baby as her mother had beaten her. "I know that's not the way to treat a child, but the impulse surges up."

A great difficulty can arise in this age period over the fact that the drive to independence is so strong that it is not an easy period in which to face emotional problems in oneself. That is why psychoanalysis is, on the whole, easier in the 30s than in the 20s. It seems to be important to suppress internal problems and concentrate on external ones. Sometimes persons in their 20s will seek analysis for anxieties, timidities, tensions or tempers in social mixing, work and family life and will make useful progress under the analysis of human relationship problems in the light of their upbringing. But they are usually keen to achieve independence of treatment prematurely, and this may well be a good thing. At 35 or later they will be in a much stronger position to sift their problems to a much deeper level, if that should prove to be necessary. [EDITORS' NOTE: *Group therapy seems peculiarly suitable for some of the adjustment problems of this decade. It capitalizes on the outgoingness of the stage, and offers the practice in interpersonal relations that so often is required for development of the new adult role.*]

As the sheer pressures of life, business and domestic, gather around them, the beginnings of a subtle loss of romance in marriage may set in. Husband and wife may drift apart through fatigue, preoccupation with their mounting responsibilities, practical anxieties concerning both work and children. Love in courtship is usually fairly free from practical pressures but can become careworn in marriage. There was a time when it could be ruined by sexual irresponsibility and the birth of too many children. Family planning is today an increasing safeguard against this. In this period of life, if people are married, they should frankly consider the limits of their capacities, not only economically but also emotionally, to cope with children and make sure their babies are wanted. Unwanted babies can occur inside as well as outside marriage, and it is inexcusable today not to face those moral obligations that arise out of a baby's right to come into the world wanted and loved.

But the threat of the wear and tear of everyday living to the romance of marriage is harder to avoid when it comes from work pressures. In an insecure and power-hungry world, not only politics but also industry and commerce are geared, with the help of technology, to a fiercely competitive system, both nationally and internationally. Just as modern education does not train women to be mothers but to compete with men for jobs, so also it does not train men to be fathers but to compete with other men for jobs. So long as fear rules our lives, human values have to take second place, but we cannot afford to be blind to this. A man and woman's marriage and freedom to love each other and their children is as important to the future of both nation and race as is economic "progress". Good technicians do not necessarily make good parents. This is urgent for the 18–30s.

One more point may be made. At 18–30 most vigorous people are optimistic, and it is easy to overestimate how much real change can be produced. Consequently, much change turns out to be external and involves little real maturing of human beings. On the other hand, older people, just because they have had time to discover this, can easily become too pessimistic, underestimate what can be done, and fail to tackle what is necessary. When young and old respect each other, the extremes can balance each other. [EDITORS' NOTE: *For many, the choice of an occupation and a mate, and making an adjustment to parenthood, are the major developmental tasks of this stage. For a further discussion, see Lidz, Chapters 12 (occupation), 13–14 (marriage), and 15 (parenthood).*]

Chapter 12

ABILITY

JOHN PARRY
Chief Psychologist to the Royal Air Force

Intelligence reaches its peak about the 16th year and when allowance has been made for individual variations we may say that its
development beyond the age of 18 is something very unusual. The
pattern is much the same for the main differentiating aptitudes—
verbal, numerical, spatial and mechanical—so that to all intents and
purposes a young man's or woman's intellectual equipment has
attained fruition by the time he or she goes to a university or com-
pletes apprenticeship to a trade. From this point of view the occupational psychologist is on safer ground assessing the capacities of 18
year olds than of boys and girls three years younger, when the possibility of late maturation cannot always be ruled out.

The maturation of aptitude is not, of course, to be confused with
the maturing of personality. Aptitude, roughly definable as potentiality for learning, develops as a natural process, its growth after
adolescence being for all practical purposes immune from the influences of the environment. Its realization in some activity can,
however, be interfered with in many ways. Thus a student's inability
to learn French or biology may result from bad instruction or from

his own failure to apply latent ability in a particular medium. All human achievement may be regarded as the product of a complex of abilities and a complex of personal factors, the instruments used by the psychologist to measure the first being distinct from those that assess the second.

Once aptitudes have reached their peak, they remain at that level for a matter of perhaps ten years, after which a gradual but initially very slight decline sets in. Hence we may regard those in the 18–30 group as at or very near the summit of their abilities. This means that, other factors being equal, they will assimilate information, make comparisons and deductions and learn new skills more quickly and surely than at any other time in their lives. Success depends, however, on their powers of selecting appropriate objectives and of pursuing them with patience, courage and persistence. The emergence and development of the latter qualities, closely related to what has become known as need achievement, cannot be plotted with the same assurance as those of the aptitudes which, so far as they are genetically endowed, tend to unfold spontaneously and at a more or less predictable tempo. The determinants of personality traits and attitudes are more complex; their roots appear to be neurological and biochemical, but there is little doubt that the quality of the earliest relationships and the attitudes of parents in the first years of the child's life play a large part in the formation of motives and the constancy with which they are followed.

This view of aptitudes derives from the body of mental testing originated by Binet at the start of the century and developed so far as Great Britain is concerned primarily by Spearman and Burt, and more recently, by Vernon. [EDITORS' NOTE: *In the U.S.A. the major contributors were Terman, Thorndike and Thurstone, and more recently Guilford.*] Tests based on this model have been standardized and validated on enormous samples drawn particularly from English-speaking populations and have supplied the backbone of almost all large-scale selection programs. Their widespread success in many armed services and industrial enterprises testifies to the basic soundness of their methodology and the solidity of their achievements.

In recent years claims have been made for a further type of test alleged to tap imaginative and creative factors hitherto neglected.

Evidence has been advanced (e.g. by Guilford, a former President
of the American Psychological Association, by Getzels and Jackson
of the University of Chicago and by Hudson of Cambridge University) to suggest that the multiple choice "convergent" item
(based on selection of the one correct answer from a number of
choices) may at some time be reinforced by an open-ended "diver-
gent" technique, which gives more scope for originality; and that
the two together may sample a wider range of abilities than is at
present possible. This evidence rests on the performance of a comparatively small number of school children and undergraduates, so
that we cannot talk with precision about the distribution of such
abilities among the general population or about their development
or decline in respect of age. There is, however, no reason to suppose
that should the independence of these abilities be substantiated, they
will be found to mature at a different time from those with which
we are more familiar.

To the student and the young man entering his first job the nagging question is likely to be "Have I the ability?", the assumption
being that if he has he can muster the will power to use it, but that
if the ability is lacking, no amount of personal effort can make up
for it. This attitude underrates the importance of interplay between
ability and personality, since the root cause of success or failure in
an occupation lies frequently in the relationship between these
rather than upon either alone, although the relative importance of
ability and personality varies to some extent from job to job (e.g.
with technicians the emphasis is on ability, with policemen on character, while with pilots the demands on both are keen and exacting).
It is not inconsistent with this to concede that in training and early
employment there is a premium on skill and learning, the emphasis
shifting in the direction of the personal qualities as supervisory duties
are assumed. From this point of view we may think of the 20s as the
decade in which intelligence and creativeness are in highest demand.
The employer, or anyway the progressive employer, will find it
harder to reject a gifted applicant for a possible personality weakness
than a sterling character for lack of sparkle.

A period of nearly full employment with a growing need for
young men with higher education appears to offer unqualified ad-

vantages to the above average schoolboy and student. Compared with 30 years ago, when many bright children could hope neither for university training nor for work worthy of their abilities, the advantages are clear enough. Nonetheless, there are qualifying factors. The very extent of the need puts pressure on the teenage child to decide on a vocation at an early age and, when from three to seven years have been invested in training him for his chosen field, a radical change of direction is made unusually difficult. In addition the demands of a scientific and technological drive are likely to foster premature talent-spotting, so that a boy of 14 with a flair for solving quadratics is apt to be cast for the role of a mathematician for which he may have little aptitude beyond computational skill. In this connection it is salutary to recall the comment of G. H. Hardy to the effect that he had reached his last year at Cambridge before he understood what mathematics was about.

It is, perhaps, inevitable that the need to fill many specialized posts should favor the possession of ready knowledge and experience as distinct from the ability to acquire and use new types of information. Thus, it is not merely difficult to change one's trade or profession, but there are forces that make for narrow typecasting within it. There is no evidence that young men are incapable of switching roles effectively; the last war yielded innumerable instances of drastic and successful changes of occupation at almost any age— accountants became successful air crew, lawyers turned into colonels, playwrights into commanders.

So far we have been considering mainly the professions and technical trades for which a high level of qualification is necessary and where, on the whole, work possesses a good deal of intrinsic interest. The bulk of these occupations carry additionally high establishment status, and broadly speaking they are in competition for the same segment of the population, namely the top 30 per cent or 40 per cent in terms of intellectual ability. These people, having undergone a lengthy training and attracted by the likelihood of reasonably early promotion, tend to remain in the line of work they set out in.

The position is somewhat different for clerical personnel, mechanics and what are loosely called semi-skilled workers. Most of these are drawn from the middle half of the population, i.e. those with Intelligence Quotients between 110 and 90. Their acceptance rarely requires more than a modest educational attainment, and training usually consists of brief on-the-job familiarization. Such work is made up for the most part of routine processes, requiring accuracy and at times speed, and its satisfaction depends to a great extent on job conditions rather than job content. Opportunities for advancement within such trades are small, and turnover is likely to be big. Many who start their vocational life in these occupations graduate to more skilled work, and the tendency is for employers to encourage those capable of improving their qualifications by further study to do so. Hence the abler young men who start to earn their living without a long preparation at university or technical college can sometimes adopt an experimental attitude to job taking which excites the envy of the more privileged. Education by job sampling is a luxury the latter find it hard to follow today once the time for vacation posts is over.

We have been speaking of the job seeker as masculine, but most of what has been said applies to girls and young women as well. The mean intelligence of women is the same as that of men, though the dispersion of ability for the latter is wider, i.e. there are more men than women with very high and very low quotients. There are differences but not extreme ones over the group abilities, women being somewhat ahead on the linguistic aspect of the verbal factors, men on the spatial and mechanical abilities. These statistical differences are of no great practical importance, being overshadowed in the practical world by the preponderance of male job seekers. The business of choosing a career normally confronts the male with a fairly straight exercise in decision-making; with the woman the question of taking work can still stir conflict, especially if it is carried to the point of choosing between career and family.

Intrinsic interest, starting pay, status and security are probably the factors influencing the majority in the choice of their careers. But there is a minority for whom the first consideration dominates all others. This group, which includes many gifted and creative people, is of great social significance since it supplies the nascent disciplines with their pioneers and stokes the fires of those undergoing a period of eclipse.

As for achievement, a glance at history quickly shows what these years have brought forth. Descartes produced his *Discourse* at 23, Einstein the Special Theory of Relativity at 25. Keats and Shelley died before their 30th birthdays, Schubert a few months afterwards. The younger Pitt became prime minister in his early 20s; Napoleon and Alexander carved empires before they were 30, and most of T. E. Lawrence's exploits were completed by the same age. Mendelssohn was a teenager with two and a half years to run when he composed the overture to *Midsummer Night's Dream*, while at 19 Rimbaud abandoned poetry to become a dock laborer. Galois, long recognized as one of the four architects of 19th century mathematics, was killed in a duel at 20, spending the hours before his last dawn covering paper with the foundations of Group Theory.

PART FIVE

Prime of Life: 30 to 42 years

*The 30s see some slackening of physical abilities, but they are
normally masked by greater experience. Emotionally there is
the risk of disillusionment for some; but others
will find this one of the happiest, most productive periods of life.*

Chapter 13

THE BODY

W. A. MARSHALL
*Lecturer in Growth and Development,
London University*

The fourth decade of human life may be regarded as its turning point. During these years the processes of growth cease to produce an obvious effect and signs of aging begin to appear. In fact growth does not stop at this time, but lasts as long as life, while breakdown and death of cells and tissues has been going on since before birth. In early life the building up process predominates, while in later years degenerative processes become relatively more important and lead to a reduction in the chemical activities and the elasticity of tissues throughout the body.

When a man is 40, the time he takes to act in sudden emergencies has already begun to increase because of aging of his brain, although his normal thought processes and his ability to learn are not greatly impaired. His greater experience may enable him to make difficult decisions more quickly.

Men in their 30s may find that they cannot read small print as well as they could because the lenses of their eyes become less elastic and thus less able to focus.

Loss of elasticity in the pelvic tissues of women makes childbirth increasingly difficult after the 30th year, because more resistance is offered to the baby's head as it passes from the uterus to the outside world. If the birth canal has already been widened by the birth of a previous child, these aging effects are much less important. In some women under 40, aging of the ovaries leads to failure to ovulate and inability to become pregnant, although there are other equally normal women who remain fertile until about 50.

The cartilages of joints begin to undergo the degenerative changes which will lead eventually to the arthritis from which all elderly people suffer to some extent. These changes are accelerated by obesity.

After the 35th year there is a decline in the amount by which the muscles can be strengthened by training. The ability to incur an "oxygen debt", and thereby continue violent exercise without an adequate supply of oxygen, remains at a maximum up to the age of about 40, while the hemoglobin content of the blood, and hence its oxygen capacity, also remains at its highest level. The efficiency of the lungs in passing oxygen to the blood is beginning to decline, but the strength and endurance are therefore at their peak in the fourth decade, although some loss of speed and agility has already taken place. At the Olympic Games athletes over 30 years of age played a prominent part in such events as long distance running, walking, weight lifting and wrestling, but more agile activities were the prerogative of younger men.

The blood pressure rises slowly but steadily in perfectly normal and healthy men between the ages of 30 and 40. This is the result of aging processes in the blood vessels. The aorta, through which blood leaves the heart for distribution to the rest of the body, is a tube about one inch in diameter with elastic walls which stretch with each beat of the heart. The elasticity of the aorta and its larger branches decreases steadily after the 25th year so that they cannot expand so easily, although the amount of blood which is pumped into them with each beat of the heart remains the same. The blood pressure at the height of the heart's contraction (the systolic blood pressure) therefore rises. The smaller arteries in the limbs are narrowed by aging processes, and the resistance to the flow of blood in the circulation as a whole is therefore increased, raising the blood pressure further. Those who are overweight in their 30s are more likely than other people to develop an abnormally high blood pressure. This may lead to prolonged impairment of health and restriction of activities in later life.

It has been suggested by some writers that many of the manifestations of aging are simply delayed effects of diseases which occurred earlier in life. Whether this is true or not there are two diseases of early life which may produce marked damage to the heart in the fourth decade, although the patient may have been unaware of their presence for many years. These are rheumatic fever and syphilis. Rheumatic fever usually occurs in childhood or early adult life, and recovery is often complete. Sometimes, however, recovery only appears to be complete and, some 15 or 20 years later, symptoms such as shortness of breath arise because the rheumatic process has affected one of the valves of the heart in such a way that it cannot open properly. Until relatively recently this condition could not be treated and led after a period of increasing breathlessness to cardiac failure and an early death. Nowadays, however, the treatment of this condition is well within the capabilities of cardiac surgeons, and the disease is no longer one to be feared. In the case of syphilis the initial illness is far milder than in the case of rheumatic fever and may be completely ignored by the victim who may not even be aware of its presence. After some 10 or 20 years, however, the syphilitic organisms may attack the heart valves and lead to heart failure and death. The treatment of syphilitic heart disease is more difficult than that of rheumatic fever and is less assured of success.

Syphilis may also affect the central nervous system causing various forms of paralysis and insanity many years after it was originally contracted.

The delayed effect of these two diseases gives rise to much speculation as to whether or not some of the phenomena which we regard as normal aging processes may not in fact be delayed effects of common diseases, but little concrete information is available on this subject. Whatever may be the cause of these so-called normal aging processes, they are clearly apparent by the age of 40 and assume an increasing importance from this time onwards.

It is in the third and fourth decades that measures to prevent or reduce the infirmity of old age must begin, and one of the simplest and most important of these is to control one's diet and take adequate exercise so that excessive gain in weight is avoided.

Chapter 14

PERSONALITY

H. V. DICKS
The Tavistock Clinic

The fourth decade is often thought of as a "settling down" period. This notion has much truth in it, but it also has an overtone of dreariness in its meaning. This decade marks the transition from youth to maturity. The ancient Greeks took 40 as this watershed. C. G. Jung had hinted at a "37-year-old crisis". There is much evidence to support the view that this phase can be as critical a challenge as adolescence—a giving up and a fear of the road ahead.

One of the symptoms of this unrest is the surprising finding of the last published British census, for 1956, which showed that the 30–40 age group had the highest divorce rate, though it is not the largest age group of marriages in the population. [EDITORS' NOTE: *The divorce rate has been steadily rising in the U.S. for the last 20 years. Currently it is at its maximum for 35–44 year old women and 45–54 year old men, while the highest percentage of married people in the American population is in the age range 35–44.*] This percentage is reflected also in attendance figures at matrimonial case work clinics. In the psychological clinic one forms some ideas of what the stresses of the fourth decade are about, and becomes convinced that personality as part of nature does not stand still but is seeking always for ways towards fulfilment and also feels threatened by inner and outer obstacles and interferences with this process.

In the preceding decade people of both sexes can be said to be largely impelled by the great impersonal life urges for survival, for fulfilling nature's tasks of livelihood seeking ("choice of career"), mating, reproduction and nest building. For the average person these tasks are now well under way. The work roles are mostly emerging as relatively stable—for men and women. In the latter it is either the married woman and mother role, or a reasonable expectation of working spinsterhood, at whatever level. [EDITORS' NOTE: *This rather astonishing view of the working woman may represent a cross-national difference. In the United States, in the last two decades, there has been a significant increase in the number of women with children who are employed, so that today more than a third of all mothers with children at home are working.*]

	% of married 1950	women 1960	working 1970
No children under 18 yrs.	30.3	34.7	42.2
Children aged 6–17 yrs.	28.3	39	49.2
Children less than 6 yrs.	11.9	18.6	30.3

We shall see that for modern women this fork in the road has its own stress points. The babies have become schoolchildren, the honeymoon flatlet a house and garden with its own demands. The first sexual torrent which cared little for environment is often now a placid stream—sometimes too placid, allowing for reflection.

The dread prospect of "settling down" then *is* the crisis. Those who pass smoothly from Spring into High Summer have no crises, even if they also have their regrets and their disappointments to meet. Most people, especially the married ones, experience this period as one of "finding themselves" in their working and married lives, gaining the confidence born of feeling no longer novices, and of the widening scope of life. This comes from professional job satisfactions, a better income, a growing together, the shared enjoyment of children's unfolding personalities—the latter perhaps the greatest source of reward for the years of early uphill struggle.

Plenty of those with difficulties in adapting to early adult life—work and marriage—are still struggling to catch up with "earlier" phases of development. But the typical emotional difficulties in this phase may be embraced by the word *disillusionment*—whether with oneself, work, marriage or life in general.

As at adolescence, unfulfilled emotional needs and potentials, put in storage while establishing one's biosocial existence, make themselves felt. The disillusionment is an awakening to the difference between youthful ideal expectations and sober reality. In a recent Chicago study the standard male response was a wish to be back to age 25, when a man was still free and eager for success. "After 35 you know you will not accomplish all you hoped to do, and you settle down into a rut." American women, on the contrary, looked to maturer years for maximum happiness.

The questioning and reflection is a symptom of the need for once again resuming the quest for wholeness and autonomy of the person so generously thrown over for mating. It is exceptional to grow so harmoniously that there is no awareness of stress. The varieties of such growing pains and solutions for them are numerous. But discontent and a sense of imprisonment in the obligations of work, marriage and parenthood, the exacting round of chores, the same faces at work and at weekends, easily lead to the search for new, exciting relationships promising once again "ideal fulfilment". Even when the real source of frustration is in one's inner sense of failure, or in slowness of promotion, or inadequacy as a mother, those nearest to one are apt to be the scapegoats on whom the anger is displaced.

This, in the married, is the spouse; in the unmarried possibly the parents or other relatives—who seem so tyrannical, unresponsive or frustrating. It is also a time of restlessness in work. In people who are apt to pass through what can justly be called a crisis in this age group (and they are a minority), the psychiatrist often finds unresolved deeper bonds attaching the person to an inner conflict with early fear- or anger-arousing parental figures. It is this continuing unconscious preoccupation with such internal feelings which constitutes the obstacle to free development, to full maturation. It is this old war which is apt to break surface again and become displaced to the significant figures of the present—the spouse, the employers, the work rivals, even the children if these seem to oust one from "coming first" in somebody's love and esteem. This is what is meant by emotional insecurity, which in the 30 to 40 age group is again to the fore, even when it was masked in the 20s during the phase of maximal biological sex drive and attack on life.

In married women, especially if they have qualifications and work experience, this is often a trying period. The children demand less but are still dependent. The woman is apt to be isolated in her dormitory suburb, the home by now a dull routine, her main reward the close comradeship and sexual devotion of her husband. But he comes, at this age, to be less entertaining, less enterprising, the more the job takes it out of him. Few men can claim to have their job as their fulfilment. This situation leads to the paradox of the less burdened wife having energy to spare, longing to be out, while the man, theoretically "in the prime of life," demands a more peaceful cherishing, has less sexual ardour and is prone to leave much of domestic decision-making to the wife. If a wife at this age is "tired," it is usually a cover for boredom or disappointment with this dreary man. Just as often she responds by donning the trousers.

We can see why in this situation a man will start dreaming of being young and having an adoring "little woman" who does not criticize and who makes him feel good, and that similar longings may insistently occupy the woman—for a gallant, enterprising lover who will make her feel attractive. So it is in people with frustrated earlier love needs that such harking back to complete happiness and support, the demand for "being all in all" to each other—and hence the disillusionment—are greatest. A wife's envy of her husband's more "interesting" daily round means she needs to vary her day and enlarge her own sphere. The husband's sense of "imprisonment" in domesticity and work often has the same basis in an idealization of the "all in all" appropriate to the youthful phase. Acceptance of the change is now required, frank facing of the "other" in their need for further growth in autonomy, for a wider network of social and cultural interests and contacts enriching and diversifying the relationship. The failure of this satisfying expansion of the circle through friends, children and quasi-professional or leisure interest groups is what makes this phase of marriage seem like bondage. "Funny," many couples in trouble have said, "when we were struggling, we were so happy—now we are better off we have nothing in common".

It is this spectacle of the threatened mutual stagnation which makes many unmarried people congratulate themselves on their "escape". It is true that the unmarried retain greater freedom of maneuver—job changes, travel, leisure pursuits and self-indulgence. But unless their single estate is the result of mature decision based on work involvement or other overriding investment of themselves in loving service, such "freedom" at this age begins to feel rather empty. They know they are missing a wealth of experience and bypassing the normal road to the fuller life. Whether still tied by care for infirm parents or to the indelible memory of a lost lover, such "alibis" often conceal a fear of commitment in sexual union.

Spinsters and bachelors are nearly always aware of their loss, even though they may have many ways of compensating themselves. Society, however, is enriched by their predicament. Where else would we find the devoted scholars, seafarers, pioneers and many artists, providing the pluralism and diversity which are a counter-weight to the "humdrum" domesticity of the majority? It would be an error to equate lasting matrimony with mental and social health, or name it as the only way to personal happiness and maturity.

The problems briefly sketched here are perhaps most marked in the higher educational and occupational groups, with their greater potential for achievement and individuality. The mass of average people have a more limited ambition and often less disturbing inner fantasy life which makes them "settle" for the sense of stability and enjoyment of the good things which at this age can still be savoured in the fullness of physical stamina and experienced mental zest, without too much existential anxiety or reaching for the stars. Much of the best work is done and the happiest moments lived in the 30s if the elders who wield power do not sabotage them.

Chapter 15

ABILITY

JOHN PARRY
Chief Psychologist to the RAF

The slight decline in intellectual ability which sets in around 25 continues during the 30s. This trend, statistically detectable through a comparison of test performances, is rarely noticeable in real life situations, largely because its effects are masked by the acquisition of experience. The loss tends to be smaller for those with high initial ability or anyway for those who exercise what abilities they have. It is the conjunction of ability still near its peak with developed poise and judgment that justifies words like prime and maturity for those in their fourth decade. [EDITORS' NOTE: *It is interesting that the results depend on the method used to obtain them. In cross-sectional studies, when different age groups are measured at a given point in time the reported decline with age is found. However, with longitudinal methods in which the same individuals are repeatedly tested as they get older, the decline with age is slight. See also Editors' note, p. 129.*]

Enquiries into the job performances of industrial workers some-times provide oblique evidence of the proficiency of those in their 30s. Thus in a recent study on the age of semi-skilled manuals, Featherstone and Cunningham found that the 25-39 group was the only one which occurred in much the same proportions in all kinds of job, whereas the over 40s supplied an unexpectedly high number in jobs entailing unfavorable conditions or severe work demands. In general, studies comparing the performances of older and younger men tend to set those over 45 against those under 35, implying that no marked degradation of skill is expected of the intermediate group.

One of the difficulties in discussing the course of the life cycle is to estimate the effects on the individual of social demands and stan-dards. While a man's raw potential is not directly touched, his atti-tude to his capabilities and the use he makes of them can be modified a great deal. This applies particularly to the learning of new skills and adaptation to unfamiliar situations. Many talk as though system-atic learning were a facility peculiar to schoolboys and undergradu-ates, and the relaxation of tempo after the mid-20s sometimes seems to confirm this belief. It takes the shock of personal or national emergency to persuade some that they retain a capacity to turn their minds and hands to new lines of activity.

While 40 marks the chronological mid-point of many careers, there are many for whom it is also the end-point of advancement. The military services, alive to the embarrassment of retaining large numbers with little prospect of promotion, frequently provide an exit point with pensions round about this age. Many professions appear to be organized as though the majority reach the peak of use-ful effort in mid-life, after which it is found pointless to stimulate them to further achievement. The fact that a minority assume higher and higher responsibility through middle and even old age suggests that this cannot be universally valid and raises the possibility that career structures are framed by other factors beside the bounds of individual capacity. [EDITORS' NOTE: *The more individualistic profes-sions—law, medicine, literature—serve as better channels for careers that continue to rise through the middle years and into later maturity. The bureaucratic occupations depend too heavily on rapid responsiveness to others and an effective meshing with an organization. Few business*

*executives in the United States extend their full employment beyond
their late 60s, while during many decades the Supreme Court justices
have had an average age close to 70.*]

The theory underlying the promotion principle is that increase in
responsibility must be recognized by increased payment. But responsibility is a complex notion, in which many strands can be discerned. When however we try to pinpoint these, it becomes difficult
to decide how far known abilities can take us and at what point we
must postulate fresh ones. We cannot, for example, yet be sure
whether judgment in complex affairs is mainly a matter of well-
applied intelligence or whether it is largely dependent, as Hearn-
shaw has suggested, on a special ability which enables a man to
structure a current situation in the light of past experience.

The ability to frame new concepts is another factor still incom-
pletely explored. There is some reason for thinking of it as an entity
in its own right, but there are as yet no highly reliable tests for assessing it. Common sense suggests that such an aptitude will be
unable to flourish unless offset by an ability to reject concepts that
have served their turn. It cannot be concluded however that the two
are opposite sides of the same coin; receptivity to new ideas does
not necessarily go with a flair for generating them. Nor does the
ability to father new ideas constitute a passport to professional success. Though lip service is paid to this talent ("Society today needs
men with ideas"), those endowed with it sometimes encounter a
form of avoidance unknown to the less gifted.

Many jobs entail increased supervisory and administrative powers
about the time the fourth decade is entered. Such duties call for
social perception, an understanding of individual capability and the
ability to delegate. Some administrators of undoubted industry and
capacity fall down over the last requirement, failing to realize that
delegation is incomplete if subordinates are continually subjected to
interruption and interference. Better an alert detachment than a
blind over-involvement.

Once the duties of management have been assumed, advancement
depends largely on the ability to think effectively over increasingly
wide areas. Thus in deciding if a man is promotable, it has to be
asked if he is capable of control and direction at the next level of

organization. If it is decided that he is unlikely to become so, he is said to have reached his ceiling. Although judgments of this sort have to be made daily, it is far from clear what sets the psychological limit to this type of growth. Superficially it may be ascribed to failure in nerve induced by the increased scope of responsibility, but even if this is descriptively sound, it does not identify the root of the failure.

The course of a career devoted to the unfolding of a single talent—acting, writing, scientific research—is hard to plot. A record of output, however factually correct, can be strangely uninforming, telling nothing about the quality of the work produced, the factors arresting development or those stimulating its advance. Close study of the life of an individual worker suggests that steady unbroken progression is very much the exception, that bursts of productivity over months or years are likely to be followed by periods of withdrawal and consolidation. The interaction of private life and public performance is another theme that inevitably eludes all but privileged observers, yet no one can imagine that the two proceed in a state of mutual insulation. The conditions favoring the release of creative ability supply a further motif on which present understanding is small.

While marriage is likely to confirm a man's choice of career and to this extent restrict his freedom to experiment, its effects, if the choice has been sound, are almost wholly positive. The claims of his job are generally accepted as transcending other claims. The professional woman is less fortunate. Quite apart from the complications brought by motherhood, the pressures of social conditioning are such that few married women can pursue a career with singlemindedness. Even when the husband is willing, as today many are, to share the domestic burden, her psychic energy remains divided, victim in a sense of her emancipation. Her difficulties are frequently enhanced by the attitudes of others, the resentment of men, the envy of many women. None of these obstacles is insuperable, but their existence means that given a man and a woman of equal ability the woman will always need that much more persistence to attain her goals. Apart from this the majority of women are temperamentally ill-equipped to face the searchlights of the public arena and the polite savagery of the professional jungle.

To the question "When does a man become too old for this or that activity?" the answer lies partly in the degree of competition from younger people and partly in the continuity of performance. Test pilots remain active into their 60s.

To recapitulate: compared with the 20s, where there is a heavy accent on vitality and raw ability, the 30s are a phase where mild decrements in performance can usually be offset by knowledge and experience. It is a decade which calls for realism and sober reckoning. Responsibilities both within the job and outside it are likely to increase, but so far as these are rewarded by increases of pay and rank they are accepted as evidence of expanding powers. Toward the age of 40 the prospect for many begins to cloud. Those who can readily harness the forces of intellect and personality will accept this as a challenge; the remainder divide rather sharply into a fair-sized group whose lives become shadowed with anxiety and a smaller number who wring achievement out of tension.

PART SIX

Middle Age: 42 to 60 years

*During middle age, physical changes
and new role expectations require adaptation.
Increasing experience offsets declining abilities.*

Chapter 16

THE BODY

W. A. MARSHALL
Lecturer in Growth and Development,
London University

The balance between physical growth and physical degeneration, which began to waver during the fourth decade, settles definitely and finally on the side of degeneration after the fortieth year, although the average man who reaches this age may expect to survive for about another 30 years and the average woman for about another 35 years. Stature begins to decline after the age of 45 or 50, and the only part of the skeleton where positive growth continues is that of the head and face, whose measurements continue to increase at least up to the age of 60. The increase between the ages of 20 and 60, however, is only some 2 to 4 per cent of the size at 20. Muscular strength and the ability to maintain maximum muscular effort both decline steadily. The loss of muscular strength is not due to a weakening of the muscle fibers themselves, but to a reduction in their number and probably to changes in the elasticity of the fibrous tissue within which the muscle fibers are embedded. By the age of 45 the strength of the back muscles in men has declined on the average to

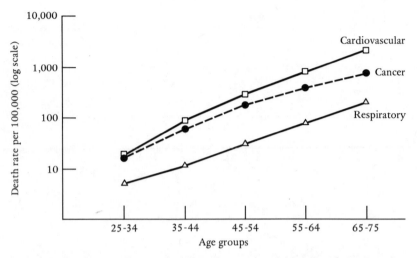

FIGURE 9. Death rates from major illnesses: young adulthood to later maturity. Note that the scale at left is logarithmic; the actual values would go far off the page if they were plotted in conventional form.

some 96 per cent of its maximum value, whereas by the age of 50 it is down to 92 per cent, and this rapid decline continues.

Men in their late fifties can only do hard physical work at about 60 per cent of the rate achieved by men of 40. Several different aspects of the aging process account for this change. As a man gets older, thickening of the walls of the minute air sacks in his lungs hinders the diffusion of gases, and he has to increase the amount of air which he breathes in order to pass the same amount of oxygen to his blood. When he is breathing as rapidly and as deeply as he can, he does not oxygenate his blood as well as he did by similar effort when he was younger.

The passage of oxygen from the blood to the working muscles is hindered in a similar way by thickening of the sheaths of connective tissue which surround the muscle fibers. The capillary blood vessels are buried in this tissue, and it becomes progressively more difficult for oxygen to diffuse from them or for waste products to diffuse from the muscle fibers to the blood. At the same time the amount of work which the muscles can do with an inadequate supply of oxy-

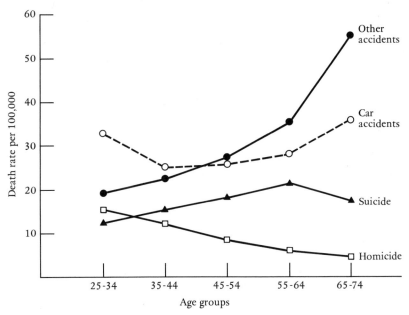

FIGURE 10. Death rates from major external causes: young adulthood to later maturity. Note the steady increase in "other accidents" as the sensory-motor processing skills gradually deteriorate. The temporary decline in "car accidents" may be a result of the compensatory benefits from practice and increased self-protective motivation to drive carefully.

gen, by incurring an "oxygen debt", is reduced, and may fall by as much as 60 per cent between the ages of 20 and 50. The amount of oxygen which the blood can carry remains near its maximum until about the age of 50 and then declines, adding further to the difficulty of supplying the working muscles. The time which a middle aged man takes to recover from hard work increases as his rate of doing work declines, so that he needs longer rests between bouts of hard work than a younger man does.

The time which people take to carry out movements increases steadily in the forties and fifties. Careful tests have shown that this slowing is not due to an inability of the muscles and joints to move quickly but to a delay in the brain and spinal cord where a longer time is required to initiate and guide the muscular activity. These changes in so-called sensori-motor activity not only reduce the rate at which skilled tasks can be carried out but also delay the individual's reaction to personal danger or other emergencies.

A man's capacity to do his accustomed work may be limited at this age by either the speed at which he can move or the amount of hard physical effort which he can tolerate, according to the nature of his job. Men in their forties usually manage, by greater skill and experience, or by greater and more continuous effort, to maintain adequate standards of work in spite of their physical limitations. The strain of doing this increases steadily however, and a point is often reached when they feel that they must change to less arduous work. They will often attribute their decision to some recent illness, but the real cause usually lies in the slow changes with age which have been accumulating over the years. The crucial age in the case of "time-stressed" jobs, such as light piecework, appears to be in the late forties and early fifties, while in the case of strenuous physical work it is in the late fifties or early sixties. If a change from heavy work is to be successful, the new lighter job must not impose a time stress. It is seldom satisfactory, for example, to transfer a middle-aged miner to assembly work in a factory. On the other hand, those who have found piece work too much for them will often be quite happy in work which is actually physically harder but where there is no longer a race against time.

The coronary arteries which supply blood to the muscle of the heart itself become narrowed and, even in apparently healthy men between the ages of 40 and 50, electrical records taken with the electrocardiograph show that the efficiency of the heart during exercise is impaired by lack of blood for its own use. In many people the blood supply to the heart muscle is reduced by this narrowing to such an extent that pain occurs during exercise. This pain is commonly known as angina of effort or angina pectoris, because it is felt in the shoulder, although it originates in the heart muscle. Narrowing of the arteries which supply blood to the muscles of the legs may cause a similar pain there. These pains are of sufficient severity to restrict the activity of the individual and so may have some protective value. Complete blockage of a coronary artery is known as acute coronary occlusion or the "sudden heart attack" which is not too uncommon in the fifth decade. Destruction of part of the muscle of the heart results from this blockage and may be sufficiently extensive to prevent the heart from fulfilling its function at all, and death results. Fortunately, however, there is often complete recovery.

The blood pressure usually rises appreciably in the fifth and sixth decades. At the menopause the blood pressure in women rises abruptly and remains a little above the male value from then on. This is only part of the general physiological upheaval which occurs at the "change of life" in women. The actual cessation of menstrual flow is usually only the final link in a chain of events which may have begun five or more years before, with aging changes and loss of function in the ovaries. Failure of ovulation and the loss of the capacity to conceive children may occur as long as two years before menstruation ceases. Various symptoms such as "hot flushes", headaches or general lack of well-being may be associated with the menopause, and there are often psychological disturbances which vary in duration and severity, but most women who are physically and mentally healthy rapidly become adapted to the changes which have taken place within them.

In men there is no dramatic change such as occurs at the menopause in women, and many men remain fertile until old age. In some there may be a loss of sexual desire, while in others there may be a renewal of sexual interest leading in some cases to bizarre forms of behavior requiring treatment. [EDITORS' NOTE: *While there are no physiological changes in men comparable to those in women, there are psychological changes in the sixth decade which may have considerable influence on sex behavior. Anxiety over reduced sexual desire and power may lead to a kind of "last fling" desperation, or to a search for new and exotic stimuli to arouse excitement. In some men, the inhibitions of earlier years appear to be relinquished in an acting-out of fantasies, sometimes involving a regression to early adolescent homosexual interests or to a fascination for teen-aged girls.*]

By the end of the sixth decade, mental activity may be noticeably impaired in some people. Thought processes are slowed down, and the memory, particularly for names, may also be impaired. These changes are partly caused by degenerative processes which affect the blood vessels of the whole body and as a result of which the supply of oxygen to the brain is somewhat reduced. This in turn may lead to damage of the brain cells themselves. In many men, however, the mental functions show little or no impairment at this age. Similarly the decline in physical ability which affects individuals of both sexes has progressed to a very different extent in different members of the aging population, so that by the age of 60 many people are anxiously waiting for retirement while others are highly active, both physically and mentally, and dread the inactivity which retirement may bring.

Chapter 17

PERSONALITY

H. V. DICKS
The Tavistock Clinic

The two decades under discussion cover 40 per cent of our population, including the greatest number of married couples in the 50-60 group. The divorce rate falls abruptly to a mere 10 per cent of all divorces. Whether this is a true index of a settled acceptance of life is hard to assess. Such a crude measure may miss those who are not enterprising or active enough to end misery by divorce, and who somehow come to terms of armed peace or sullen resignation. We do know that in this age group depressive illnesses show an increased incidence in both sexes, alcoholism takes root, stress disorders such as coronary disease take increasing toll, and liability to physical illnesses and aging processes rises also. These well-known hazards of middle age bring with them some growth in anxiety and worry about health, and the beginnings of awareness of death—hence perhaps also a greater interest in religion and philosophy and the consolations they may offer. We need only observe who form the bulk of church congregations.

Attitudes toward work and major new enterprises and change are also mixed. While our society is ruled by the elderly, it also proclaims the doctrine of "too old at forty". Except in the learned professions, in senior posts in industry, business, and politics (accounting for a tiny upper crust), both men and women employed by others tend now to reach a level above which, apart from increments and minor changes, they will not rise. They do their best and carry the responsibilities which earn the eulogies and gold watches at the end. But they may feel a deadly monotony from which escape into new work is much harder than in the preceding decade. Much depends on their having surmounted the 37-year-old crisis described in the previous chapter. Yet it is, after all, only a minority who suffer the inner conflicts that check maturity and the living out of the normal roles and functions of each age. For the majority, not too absorbed with psychological conflicts and their effect on mental and physical well-being, middle age can indeed be a very happy, busy time. "Life begins at 50" is no empty jest which merely covers the dread of aging. Its significance will vary with sex, married or single status, and class and employment levels.

For women there is the obvious "crisis" point of the menopause or change of life when nature unmistakably decrees the end of physical motherhood. It is traditionally held to be a time of instability, and thus serves as a respectable peg on which to hang many emotional difficulties occurring between 40 and 60! A woman's reaction to the bodily discomforts and the end of reproductive powers which the menopause brings will depend greatly on her psychological readiness to taste the freedom and status society accords its seniors. This means that, single or married, she has developed a sense of worth and identity which does not need to be shored up by purely biological assets. This is often easier for the married with the evidence of their achievements in the now adult children and grandchildren who also provide lasting outlets for maternal impulses and affection. Indeed, it is when teenage rebellion is over that a woman receives perhaps the greatest reward from the thanks of her children, who now know what it has all meant, and from the unalloyed because intermittent pleasure of being the wholly benign and *never* angry grandmother. She may also have greater leisure, ampler funds and modern aids to keeping trim, handsome and well-groomed. If so, whether she finds this part of life satisfying or burdensome, depends on a woman's inner freedom to use these advantages in work, public service or sociability. The Chicago women in the survey reported in Chapter 16 favored the forties and fifties, because of their freedom.

This freedom almost certainly includes the freedom from further risks of pregnancy after the menopause, when sexual life with a still virile husband can be fully enjoyed for its continued expression of loving intimacy in a cosy, secure way; or when, in the later years, it becomes less of a problem for both sexes unless they cling to the fantasy that sex is the sole expression of continued vigor and fun in life. This pre-occupation is perhaps commoner in men of this age group. Such is the link between naive self-esteem, successful achievement and sexual potency, that any impairment in one of these can seriously damage either of the other two. Men at this age are touchy and jealous about promotion, about younger rivals displacing or overtaking them. They worry and overwork in consequence, and also feel hurt by their wives' greater independence and possible sexual indifference.

The beginnings of the subtle shift in power relations between men and women occurred, as we saw, some ten years earlier. The normal and reasonably mature of both sexes accept it and iron out the clashes to which it periodically leads within a framework of mutual tolerance and respect. A majority of Anglo-Saxon men are consciously reconciled to the greater wisdom and control over them by their wives, and the latter usually know how to avoid wounding their man's *amour-propre*. It is not unusual for a middle-aged woman to be proud of her husband's public achievements and image while at home he is content to be spoilt and sometimes bossed like a little boy. Only when neither sex can accept such a situation do real tensions and bitterness arise.

Both sexes are now apt to be less flexible; habits are more set, and awareness of the difficulties of major upheavals is greater. While the top one or two per cent of people in the highest intelligence and social strata retain greater mental agility and freedom to change their lives, for them major change is connected with more risk of public shame or loss of status—whether it be a divorce or leaving a safe job. We rightly admire people who have the resilience to "start again" in their fifties. The relative fixity of this age favors "stability", but it also increases the sense of imprisonment which is the result of a rigidity born of emotional insecurity.

Clinging to roles which were appropriate in younger days deforms the process of growing older graciously and lovably. It produces the devouring need to possess her children and be the center of her husband's attention in the middle-aged woman who develops hysterical or depressive behavior around the menopause and suspects her husband of infidelity, because he cannot show love for and sexual interest in a nagging, suspicious shrew but resolutely has his nose to the grindstone. It produces the man whose greed for power is his reassurance against a secret dread of waning capacity, and who cannot concede independence to his sons and hence to his younger colleagues, and who crabs innovation if it does not come from him. His anger and depression stems from the gap between the still rigidly held image of the ideal and the reality, leading to rejection of the latter. In the more conscientious and educated this usually leads to withdrawal and feeling henpecked; in the more primitive to drinking and angry outbursts, thus justifying the wife's nagging.

If the task of the thirties was adaptation to disillusionment, the challenge of middle age is *resignation*—giving up one's omnipotence wishes and gaining a sense of perspective of one's own place and power to influence the course of events. For both sexes, whether they be single or grandparents, this is the crisis point of growth or of regression. If they accept resignation, they can enter into the enjoyment of "life at 50", with the occasional nostalgia for lost youth which they may share and which all mankind understands.

Resignation can lead to secure contentment, "cultivating one's own garden", hobbies and cultural interests. It can also end worry about oneself and free one's energies for the tasks and roles which society assigns to this age group: to be the power holders and teachers and master craftsmen of their generation, to man the councils and lead the democratic processes. This means that to some extent the narrow domestic loyalties to one's primary family or reference group now broaden into parental concern for the larger welfare, even if for each individual concerned this may seem to be an expression of his ambition or enlightened self-interest. Society needs this. It is when such a development has failed that we get the domestic tyrants, the choleric outbursts and the strokes and coronaries; and also the depressive states of vain regrets and self-condemnation, or the pathetic attempts to deny these by desperate love affairs and pseudo-youthfulness which contain their own retribution.

At its best, this is the fullest and richest phase of all. And even at its average it brings a good harvest and a flowering of social and personal maturity—which is wisdom. [EDITORS' NOTE: *For a thoughtful discussion of the problems of adaptation to middle age, see Lidz, Chapter 16.*]

Chapter 18

ABILITY

R. M. BELBIN
Consultant on aging
OECD

Aging is the process of maturation and decline. But it is not a simple process, and the human capacity for adjustment is such that most forms of decline are matched by compensations. In many societies advancing age enjoys a reputation for increased wisdom and status. In the United States those in the age span under review, 42-60, often bear the title "mature adults"—a description parallel to "senior citizens" which is commonly applied to those over 60. These desirable terms suggest the ideal state which these ages convey.

In a sense the maturity of those in their forties and fifties is justified by the evidence. All the abilities which are likely to develop throughout life have fully matured by the forties and fifties while, except for those suffering from physical or mental ill-health, few significant and well-established abilities have been impaired by age.

Experimental studies of age in relation to various measures of skill and ability, however, suggest that important differences in trend

exist between different classes of ability. It is necessary to differentiate between abilities that are closely tied to the efficiency of senses
and organs, and which are likely to prove critical as in sport, and
complex abilities or skills, the exercise of which is relatively free
from the limitations imposed by any particular physical function.
Another distinction that must be drawn is between well-maintained,
well-practiced abilities and abilities that have not been exercised or
which make unfamiliar demands.

Insofar as abilities relate to the basic activities underlying human
performance—i.e. in efficiency in seeing or hearing; in ability to
associate and to recall; and in the maximum power of muscle movement—there are strong grounds for reckoning that the age span
42-60 is one accelerating decline. The rates of decline vary with
the measures chosen. Many tests of the efficiency of sensory processes show decline to occur from about 20. Often the decline is
earlier; for the upper frequency limits of hearing, for example, loss
of ability occurs from about 10 years of age. By the ages 45-50, a
50 per cent loss in efficiency from the age of peak performance is
recorded on a wide range of tasks that have been the subject of laboratory studies, such as line-drawing through a mirror; identification
of incomplete pictures briefly exposed; or learning of English-Turk-
ish vocabulary. Other abilities more akin to those in everyday use
have shown less decline.

Some abilities which are considered especially prone to decline
with old age show relatively little impairment in middle age. Thus,
short-term memory span, as measured by immediate repetition of
a number of digits, shows very little loss with age in the forties and
fifties. Only a small loss of efficiency, too, is shown in speed of
movement in reaction time tests, although interpretation of signals,
preceding movement, is markedly slower. In fact, the most marked
losses generally seem to occur in handling incoming information
where this is complex and unfamiliar and has to be handled at speed.
Learning to operate a power sewing machine in a factory or learning to drive a car are everyday examples of situations associated with
increased difficulty and loss of performance by the 40s and 50s.

The ability to maintain skills once acquired, on the other hand,
is very remarkable. It is proverbial that people never forget how to

FIGURE 11. Abilities in the age range 42–60.

I. established complex skills (example: mathematical and scientific ability) well maintained.
II. established lower order skills in which some basic ability can limit performance (example: tennis, swimming) slight loss
III. basic abilities—efficiency of senses and limbs (example: tree felling) usually moderate loss
IV. ability to acquire skill, especially in unfamiliar, complex, or time stressed situations (example: learning to operate a high speed machine) Usually appreciable loss

swim or how to ride a bicycle. "Knowing how" is something that seems immune to the depredations of aging. This manner of knowing is something that grows with experience and is consolidated by a wide range of short cuts and special techniques for achieving goals. Skill and knowledge of this type usually afford ample protection from any limitations imposed by the basic processes of aging.

Therefore, it is useful to conceive of abilities as falling into four broad groups, as shown in Figure 11.

The implications of these changes in ability in occupational life are far reaching. Those with Group I abilities continue to flourish. As very little of their acquired skill is lost, they gain in stature and occupy the pre-eminent positions in industrial, commercial and professional life. For those with abilities in Group II, factors of physical health and well-being begin to assume significance. On the other hand those who have acquired neither Group I nor Group II abilities are obliged to compete in occupational life on the basis of Group III and IV abilities in which a growing inferiority is likely. Hence, those who lose their jobs in the age range 42-60 and lack transferable skills find themselves at appreciable disadvantage in finding new employment. They tend to take on work that is uncongenial or less well paid. In times of unemployment they are particularly susceptible to the effects of age discrimination. In depressed areas the hard core unemployed are predominantly persons in the latter half of working life.

Middle age, therefore, brings about a wide divergence of fortunes which can partly be ascribed to the way in which abilities change with age. The more able tend to consolidate and extend their knowledge and skills (for their skills are comparatively resistant to impairment by aging), and the less able, or those less favored by opportunity, tend to show a decline in abilities never fully developed or exercised.

These generalizations concerning abilities and age, however, demand certain supplementary comments. In laboratory studies of human performance a marked tendency has been noted for increasing dispersion to occur in performance scores in the forties and fifties. A minority of persons at these ages on a wide range of tasks produce scores typical of persons in their twenties. Average scores may decline for those tested in different age groups, but averages can be misleading when a substantial minority do not follow the average pattern. These "exceptions" serve to discount biological aging as the sole or even prime determinant of performance changes over a wide range of abilities, especially where abilities comprise a modicum of skill. Where biological changes with age exercise an over-riding influence, as for example on the acuity of the senses, the effects are quite different: age changes follow a more consistent and predictable pattern. [EDITORS' NOTE: *For a detailed longitudinal study of the interests, abilities and personality qualities of a highly intelligent sample of nearly 1500 Californians, from age 11 to 45, see Terman and Oden (1959).*]

Another significant point is that abilities do not simply grow and wane. They change also in their quality. This is made evident from many studies where both speed and accuracy of performance have been measured. The older performer inclines towards accuracy at the expense of speed. He is averse to errors and mistakes and will spend more time on checking. Work surveys have shown that he is a better timekeeper and generally more reliable than his younger counterpart. The middle-aged and older worker shows a preference for certain classes of industrial occupation. He tends to move away from speed stressed machine operations and jobs linked by conveyor belts and shows an inclination for jobs where checking is an important feature, such as inspection or storekeeping.

In short, it would appear that there are important changes in the "norms" of ability in the forties and fifties. Many of these changes are due to complex interactions of biological and environmental forces, and it is only the overall result which we can record. Thus, we cannot be sure how far changes with age in ability are attributable to our pattern of living.

For most people life after infancy is divided into two sharply separated periods. The first period comprises full-time education and vocational training, terminating in the 'teens or early twenties. In the second period learning is abandoned for gainful employment, and henceforth people continue to practice what they know. We cannot be certain how far this rigid separation of stages contributes to the decline in adaptability and learning capacity which tends to become evident in the forties and fifties.

In recent years facilities for the vocational training of middle-aged adults have been greatly expanded in the countries of Western Europe and North America on the recommendations of the Organization for Economic Cooperation and Development. A new pattern is arising of a broader-based vocational education and better opportunities for changing jobs at various periods throughout working life. If and when this pattern becomes established, the habits and abilities of those in the age range 42-60 might well undergo significant changes. But many shibboleths will need to be discarded before developing facilities result in a real extension of opportunity for middle-aged adults in employment.

PART SEVEN

Old Age: Beyond 60 years

The last scene of all, in our book of life, shows that old age can be far removed from "second childishness and mere oblivion". Yet we must prepare for, and face, its problems.

Chapter 19

THE BODY

W. A. MARSHALL
*Lecturer in Growth and Development,
London University*

The period of human life which begins at 60 may be called the age of uncertainty. Perhaps the most uncertain thing about it is its length. On average, men who reach their 60th birthday may expect to live for another 14.5 years, while the average 60 year old woman may expect to survive until she is about 76.5. A great many of these, however, will die before they are 70, and a few will survive beyond the century mark. The maximum span of life, that is the age beyond which an individual could not live even under the most favorable conditions, is not known. Men have certainly lived for 114 years.

The health, strength and ability of people over 60 varies as much as the length of their lives, and there must be similar flexibility in the arrangements which are made to provide them with occupations or care. Decline at senescence, like growth at adolescence, is a matter of many individuals following similar patterns or change at different rates, and it is as hit or miss to think about legislating for the aged in terms of their chronological ages, as it is to plan the education and activities of the young on this basis. The problem is made

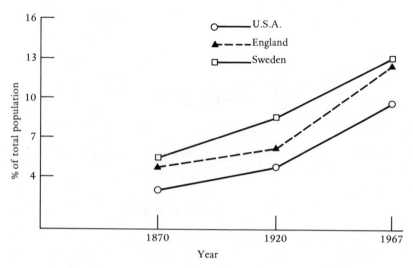

FIGURE 12. Later maturity: the percentage of the total population aged 65 and older. All three countries have been increasing the number of "aged" during the last century, but the United States still has the smallest proportion.

even more difficult in the elderly, because it is hard to distinguish clearly between normal old age and the effects of illness both past and present.

True physiological old age, that is complete freedom from the effects of disease, is agreed to be rare, and it may not occur at all. Speaking statistically, we know that as people become older they are more likely to die. Speaking physiologically, we know that the tissues of old people become less capable of carrying out their functions. This loss of function is due partly to degenerative changes in the active cells themselves and partly to an increase in the amount of inactive fibrous tissue by which they are surrounded. Cells which do not divide during life, such as those of the brain, may gradually deteriorate and become less fit for their job. In tissues whose cells divide there may be changes which cause the daughter cells resulting from a division to be less well adapted to their task than the parent cell from which they were derived. These statements are, however, purely descriptive and bring us little nearer to understanding the cause of aging. Because chicken cells in carefully controlled culture media can divide actively and without any apparent loss of vigor for many years, it has been suggested that cells themselves do not age, and only changes in their environment lead to their degeneration and ultimate death. [EDITORS' NOTE: *The apparently unlimited division may result from an artifact in the experimental procedure. Recent research suggests that cells can only undergo a limited number of divisions.*] This could mean in effect that the aging of any cell in the body is due to the aging of the rest of the body, and that the aging process as a whole is a sort of chain reaction in which one adverse change causes another, although the nature of the initial change is unknown and may not be the same in all individuals.

Aging affects all the structures and functions of the body. The mechanisms for protection against infection and for adaptation to change deteriorate as age advances. While strength and endurance decline, the memory is also failing, and thought processes are subject to change just as much as are repair mechanisms and nutritional requirements.

The strength of the forearm muscles as shown by the force and duration of the grip is about the same in men aged 75 to 80 as it is in boys just before their adolescent strength spurt. A healthy man of about 70 can perform moderate physical work with the same mechanical efficiency as a man of about 40 and, if both men were to do the hardest work of which they were capable, the heart rate and respiration rate would rise by about the same amount in both of them. In spite of this, the older man would only achieve about 50 per cent of the amount of work of which the younger one was capable, because, with aging, the body is less able to adapt itself to the needs of violent exercise. The metabolic rate of the tissues and the amount of sugar in the blood cannot increase by the requisite amount. The lungs are less efficient in saturating the blood with oxygen, while the blood itself cannot carry so much oxygen, even when it is saturated because the amount of hemoglobin which it contains has become reduced. Because the heart and blood vessels have undergone degenerative changes, they are less able to supply blood to the active tissues, while these tissues themselves are less efficient in using such oxygen as they do receive. The heart rate and blood pressure remain raised for a much longer time after exercise has ceased in elderly people than in the young.

Changes in posture also have a much more marked effect on the circulatory system in the aged. On suddenly changing from a lying to a standing position, there is a drop in blood pressure followed by an increase in heart rate which causes the blood pressure to return to normal. In old people the drop in blood pressure is much greater, but the heart rate does not increase so much. Recovery, therefore, takes longer, and in the meantime the brain may be sufficiently deprived of blood to cause a feeling of faintness or actual loss of consciousness. The reduced ability to react quickly to postural changes is an important factor in limiting the activities of some elderly people.

The declining capacity of the elderly for violent exercise is generally recognized, but there are other more important changes which are often ignored. The response to external stimuli and injurious forces becomes slower and weaker, while repair following injury is also slowed. In terms of everyday life these changes mean that the aging person reacts less violently to infection or other injuries and develops milder symptoms and signs of disease. As a result, illnesses are often well advanced in older people before they seek medical advice. The fact that older persons tolerate extreme heat or cold poorly is also due to their diminished physiological response to adverse environmental conditions.

Because adaptability is lessened in old age, under-eating, over-eating, dehydration or too rapid fluid intake are liable to lead to much more serious consequences than in youth. The general metabolism decreases, and the total requirement for food therefore becomes less; but there is a decreasing margin of safety in regard to deficiency of certain elements, and a diet of high quality, rich in proteins, minerals and vitamins is as necessary in old age as in childhood.

Both hearing and sight tend to deteriorate as age advances. Hardening of the lens of the eye, with the resulting difficulty in focussing, increases and is often accompanied by a brownish discoloration which causes further impairment of vision. Sometimes the lens becomes increasingly opaque, and complete loss of vision ultimately results from this condition, known as cataract. The commonest form of cataract is not apparently the result of any ocular or general disease and must be regarded as a continuation of the normal processes of degeneration associated with old age. Impairment of vision is often the most important factor limiting the activity of otherwise healthy elderly people, and in combination with their decreasing ability to react quickly in emergencies, it is the main cause of their proneness to accidents on the road and in the home.

Cerebral function in general does not deteriorate as rapidly in old age as many people imagine, unless degenerative processes in the cerebral arteries are unusually advanced. Thought may lose some of its speed and clarity; but where there have been good powers of judgment in early life, these continue to benefit from experience. Where there is a will to learn, the ability to do so may be as high at the age of 80 as it was at 12.

Some pathological changes are so closely associated with old age that even if they are not part of the normal aging process they must be considered in any study of the later years of life and must be born in mind by those who wish to make plans for the welfare of the elderly. The most important of these are arteriosclerosis, hypertension, arthritis and the various cancers. These diseases have certain important characteristics in common. They begin insidiously and may progress without symptoms for several years before subjective physical stress or observations by a medical adviser draw attention to the fact that something is wrong. Both preventive measures and treatment must therefore be applied before disease is apparent. Most cancers are now amenable to treatment if they are recognized early enough, but the elderly are usually unwilling to seek medical advice about what appear to them to be minor symptoms. None of these diseases of senescence has a readily identifiable cause, such as a germ, and they may be due to a variety of factors which originate within the body as well as outside it. This is another obstacle to effective prevention. Their presence tends to increase the vulnerability of the victim to other illnesses, particularly infections such as pneumonia. The course of all these diseases is such that they tend to lead to a prolonged period of disability before death results either from them or from another cause such as an acute infection.

There are many men of 65 whose strength, skill and mental abilities have deteriorated to such an extent that they are unfit to carry on their accustomed way of life and are suited only for a leisurely retirement, which may soon deteriorate into invalidism. On the other hand, there are many men of 75 who are capable of a moderate amount of physical work and in some cases of a considerable amount of intellectual work. Nothing is gained by either these men or the community if they are forced into a premature retirement simply because they happen to have lived for more than six and a half decades.

Senescence and death mark the end of a process of growth which, since middle life, has been fighting a losing battle with the forces of degeneration but is carried on with steadily increasing vigor in succeeding generations.

Chapter 20

PERSONALITY

FELIX POST
*The Bethlehem Royal Hospital
and the Maudsley Hospital*

Changes of personality during the Seventh Age of Man are frequently portrayed by poets, dramatists and novelists. Depending on the author's outlook and purpose, elderly persons are either caricatured or idealized. Similar attitudes can be discerned in psychiatrists and psychologists. Some, under the impact of clinical experiences, stress decline and deterioration; others, basing themselves largely on the life histories and later productions of outstandingly gifted and creative persons, try to make us believe that personality developments can occur during old age which transcend levels reached during maturity.

In recent years, a beginning has been made in the conduct of more scientific studies of the aging personality by workers who have learned to make allowances for their own attitudes and bias. These investigations have mostly been cross-sectional: they have compared samples of the elderly population with matched groups of younger persons in terms of their responses to various questionnaires and inventories. The main disadvantage of this approach is obviously that people belonging to different generations have been inculcated with different values, beliefs and attitudes. To give but one example, some studies suggest that religious beliefs are strengthened with increasing age, while other samples have failed to confirm this. Recently, the results of longitudinal studies, in which the same aging persons have been repeatedly assessed over a number of years, have begun to come in. But we must remember that all changes are minimal alterations and shifts of emphasis, which are overshadowed by the continuity of personality and character throughout life. As we have lived, so we grow old.

Old people prefer not only those interests and activities which are less demanding and less strenuous, but also those which are pursued in small groups, with one other person, or on one's own. Competitiveness is avoided, present achievements are accepted and the past is regarded with satisfaction. On the other hand, rigid conservatism and unwillingness to accept new ideas and changes are characteristics of old age which have been somewhat exaggerated. During the seventh decade, which may be looked upon as a transitional period preceding real old age, anxiety and worrying restlessness are often encountered, but later on stresses, bereavements, restriction through ill health, and even the proximity of death are less and less apt to produce disturbances.

On the other hand, people, as they grow older, tend to take an increasing interest in the functions of their bodies. This may seem understandable, as most elderly persons do, in fact, suffer from multiple physical handicaps and disorders, were it not for the frequency with which real disease is ignored, while attention is directed toward unaffected organ-systems, especially the functionings of the bowels. This preoccupation, an increased prevalence of food fads, rigid adherence to habits and customs, and parsimony are among the many characteristics of the senile personality which have been attributed by many workers to libidinal regression from genital to pregenital (largely anal) levels. This view is made plausible by the fact that decline of sexual (genital) drives is one of the outstanding features of the post-reproductive period of life.

Other mechanisms may be equally important in producing senile changes. Only a small proportion of elderly people are usually regarded as fully preserved in terms of the North Atlantic stereotype of the well-adjusted person: alert, outgoing, active in various organizations, gregarious and modishly dressed. The great majority of aging people lose what few contacts they had outside their family, and even within the family there occurs a process of progressive disengagement. There is a gradual change from mutually love-seeking relationships to those of dependency, and old people finally tend to take little interest in other persons other than with reference to their own diminishing needs.

Occupational retirement is often regarded as an arbitrarily enforced kind of disengagement. However, on analysis it is usually found to be the result of ill health and due to employer's action in only 25 per cent of men. Even under these circumstances, disengagement is mostly a graduated process during periods of full employment, when temporary or part-time jobs are available. In the case of women, occupational disengagement is even more gradual, and they usually remain engaged in a network of mutual services with daughters and granddaughters. Following retirement, men tend to become more isolated than women and, perhaps as a kind of compensation, they like to indulge in sweeping statements and judgments unrestrained by fears of criticism.

Personality changes in old age may be derived from libidinal regression, but they can also be understood as a result of social processes. In addition, investigators of cognitive changes in old age have pointed out that many characteristics of old persons, such as narrowing of interests, restriction of activities, difficulties in decision-making and rigidity, could all be the result of deterioration of neuro-chemical mechanisms, which serve short-term storage of information and learning processes. Whatever the cause, all personality changes have the same result: increasing introversion and decreasing communication with the outside world.

This turning inwards with increasing age may be regarded as a "good thing" in terms of biological adaptation. Under natural conditions, animals rarely outlive their ability to reproduce themselves, and their continued existence as so many useless mouths to feed would impair the chances of survival of their species. In our society, however, the old can be useful. Man and some of his precursors evolved the use of symbols (especially language) and thus the ability to code, store and transmit information. With their aid, the old began to play an increasingly important role of elaborating information in symbolic form and of passing it on to the next generation. Finally, with increasing civilization they came to provide stabilizing leadership in spite of waning physical strength.

In these functions, as grandparents at the lowest level, or as senators at the highest, many youthful characteristics, such as outgoing aggressiveness, competitiveness, sexuality, or an eagerness and ability to integrate every new impression would prove a hindrance. On the other hand, a certain degree of aloofness, disengagement from demanding relationships, and wisdom harvested from earlier years, all present assets. Thus, personality changes in old age may make a person singularly well-adapted for this period of life, and the characteristics of elderly people, like so many other biological variables, may well be the results of evolutional and selective pressures.

Yet nature has not succeeded completely. Mythology, fiction, and history contain many examples of struggles between the young and the old. Furthermore, the aging personality is much exposed to unfavorable influences. Too much has probably been made of the stresses derived from modern social conditions—industrialization, urbanization, changes in family structure, mores and attitudes. More important and, in the very old often fatal, is bereavement through loss of spouse. Unfortunately, the elderly are especially prone to suffer from degenerative brain change leading to irreversible impairment and finally to destruction of all personality functions (the dementias).

Finally, people who have always shown excessive self-preoccupation and difficulties in communicating with others may develop disabling personality changes as the result of further introversion, sexual regression, and disengagement. The shy and unsociable may become senile recluses; those who have always anxiously preserved their belongings, misers; and those who have always been anxious about their physical states, hypochondriacs. Worriers may develop frequent depressions and abnormal fears as they grow old, and sensitive, suspicious persons may show persecutory preoccupations. Sexual misdemeanors of old men can usually be traced to some earlier, often minor, sexual maladjustments. Physical deterioration and disease, social stresses, loss of family support, and flaws in personality structure, all these combine to make old age the period of life during which there is the heaviest incidence of minor and major mental disorders. Yet, even within the highest age ranges, the majority of old people remain well-adjusted to their life situation and to their society.

Chapter 21

ABILITY

A. T. WELFORD
Fellow of St. John's College, Cambridge

The decade from 60 to 70 is, more than any other during the adult years, a time of transition. Many changes of body and mind, of capacity and attitude, which have been continuous since the early twenties now have become critical, not only for work but also for some facets of daily living. In this decade most people finally give up full-time paid employment and begin to face the pleasures and problems of retirement. For many, the later 60s see the beginning of a need, which becomes increasingly common in the 70s, for various kinds of help and care during the last years of life.

In short, the 60s mark the passage from middle to old age, bringing a range of demands and challenges to the individuals concerned which they have never had to meet before.

Changes in sensory capacity, muscular strength and especially central brain function have many effects. Decision and control of action become slower, so that a man in his 60s may take twice as long to make a coordinated, visually guided movement as a man in

his 20s. Immediate memory becomes poorer, not so much because
the amount that can be retained for short periods is reduced, but
because the traces storing the data tend to be more easily disrupted
by any other activity taking place during the period of retention.
There is difficulty in searching the material stored in long-term
memory due, seemingly, to reduced ability to shift rapidly from
one area of search to another. Intelligence test scores, which rise
to a peak in the late 'teens or early twenties, have returned in the
sixties to the level they were at the age of about 10. [EDITORS' NOTE:
*A comparison of gross mental age scores can be misleading, because, as
the author points out, the patterns of abilities at the early and late ages
are very different. Furthermore, recent research has thrown doubt on the
findings that overall scores decrease as radically with age as these figures
imply. There is evidence that average intelligence test scores among
Americans are rising from one generation (i.e., age cohort) to the next,
presumably because of vastly widened education at the elementary and
high school levels. To reiterate a general point made in the "Personality" section above: cross-sectional studies of different age groups necessarily draw samples from populations that were not originally equal
in intelligence test scores. Longitudinal data, i.e., repeated tests on a
single group through the life span, are needed to determine the effects
of aging. In the Terman Gifted Group there was evidence of a significant increase in score from age 30 to 42 (Terman and Oden, Chapter
5). In another investigation, a modified longitudinal study of 10 age
cohorts, from 20 to 70 years, who were retested after 7 years, it was
found that the cross-sectional comparisons yielded far more severe decrements with age than did those derived from the longitudinal measures.
(See Schaie and Strother, in P. Sears (Ed.) Chapter 1, Section 3).*]

As against these losses, the subject's stock of knowledge is at least
maintained and often continues to mount: vocabulary scores, for
example, are usually at least steady from the 30s onwards, and often
tend to rise at later ages.

Acquisition of new knowledge seems clearly to become more
difficult in old age, but the difficulty is more in comprehending what
has to be learned and in holding it in short-term memory long
enough for more permanent memory traces to be established, than
in sheer inability to register new data. Given suitable conditions for

understanding and for learning at an appropriate pace, older people
seem to master new material surprisingly well. Their mastery is
sometimes greater than appears at first sight: for example, in one
study people over the age of 60 were found less able than those of
student age to describe in words road safety posters they had been
shown, but were equally able to use the data contained in the posters
as a basis for comment on photographs of street scenes. They had,
in short, acquired more from the posters than they could readily put
into words. Much of the difficulty that people *feel* with regard to
learning in later years is probably exaggerated and due to their
trying to master new tasks too quickly—they often try to achieve in
half an hour what would have taken them many hours during school
or student days.

The more adverse changes with age are sometimes the result of
disease and can be reversed by appropriate medical care, but for the
most part they are due to physical changes of the organism, including the brain, which regularly come with passing years. Such
changes are not the only factors affecting performance by older
people, however, but are supplemented by, and interact with, effects
of experience during life and with circumstances which tend to
change as a man or woman becomes more senior. Thus, for example,
experience of success and failure during life can greatly affect attitudes to particular activities in old age, and relief from the expense
of bringing up a family when it has moved away from home is likely
to reduce the need to earn. Again the effectiveness with which a task
can be performed in later years will depend very much upon the
balance between requirement for the kind of mental agility assessed
by measures such as intelligence tests and demand for accumulated
knowledge. When the latter predominates, an older person will
show the "wisdom" of age; when the former, he will tend to show
"rigidity".

Controlled studies designed to ascertain the nature of work suitable for men and women over 60 are rare. Broadly, the factors
making work suitable or unsuitable for those in the late forties and
fifties become accentuated. Older people often appear to do well in
professional and highly skilled occupations, but achievement at these
has so far proved impossible to measure with the same accuracy and
confidence as semi-skilled work. Two examples of the successful

employment of older men at a wage-earning level can, however, be quoted. First, an engineering firm retained skilled tradesmen past retiring age to make spare parts for obsolete machinery. The men had been employed on the construction of these machines when in current production, and the knowledge they had thus gained gave them an advantage over younger men. Second, a bakery firm, short of teenage labor as assistants to delivery van drivers, recruited pensioners. The work was active although not strenuous, and while not intellectually exacting, placed a premium on tact and other human qualities in which the older men were at an advantage.

These examples, although of limited applicability, illustrate the important general principle that the strongest claims of older people to employment are commonly in terms of skill, knowledge and human qualities such as reliability and tact.

The fundamental physical changes of old age cannot be reversed, but a great deal can be done to shape the conditions of life for older people so that they can use the powers that remain to the fullest advantage. Thus, relatively minor modifications to some industrial jobs could profoundly affect their suitability for older people. Several spontaneous and seemingly unconscious changes of behavior also tend to optimize performance in later years. For example, the tendency among old people to be accurate and meticulous can often largely compensate for slowness, because less time is wasted correcting errors. This is especially so with craft work where one error may make scrap of an article that has taken many hours to fashion: other examples could doubtless be found in a wide range of industrial work if sufficiently detailed studies were made. Probably the restriction of interest in old age and increased reliance on established routine can be regarded as ways of shedding part of what would otherwise be an undue load of physical and mental activity.

The essential result of all these tendencies is that, as age advances, the *method* and *manner* of performance change more than its effectiveness. They also lead to subtle changes of personality and way of life, which are seldom easy to demonstrate scientifically, but can perhaps be illustrated in the kinds of accidents sustained by older people: there is a clear shift with age from accidents attributable to carelessness or lack of skill, to those resulting from slowness of reaction or judgment.

The main social importance of changes in capacity with age lies in their relation to retirement and to the need for care and support. To these problems we now briefly turn.

Individuals age at different rates, so that variation of capacity between one person and another tends to rise with age. Any fixed retiring age—say at 65—will thus inevitably be too early for some and too late for others. Flexibility of retirement age, even if administratively inconvenient, is needed if the full work potentiality of those in their 60s and beyond is to be realized: the flexibility does not, however, need to be very great; a range from 60-75 would suffice for almost all employed persons.

To view the matter in perspective, it must be remembered that final retirement from full-time work is only one of a series of adjustments which go on during adult life, often bringing about one or more changes of job in middle age. Fast, or very strenuous, work will have been abandoned in the late 40s or early 50s in favor of work which may still demand considerable physical effort, but where the pace is under the operator's own control. Although trade and craft skills are well maintained in later years, production jobs, especially those involving complex machinery, will have been surrendered in favor of maintenance work, where the operator is freer to set his own methods of working. Formal retirement often does not mean the end of all work. Many continue with part-time jobs, either paid or voluntary, or continue something like a working interest in a hobby. Such activities are widely, and probably rightly, regarded as aiding adjustment to retirement by providing a framework to life and an interest beyond self. They are also likely to help preserve capacities by encouraging effort and giving opportunity for the exercise of skills.

It is worth noting that many skills and activities learned when young can be revived in old age with relatively little trouble—much less than would be involved in learning them from scratch when old.

It is generally agreed that considerations of mental and physical health, as well as of economic factors, favor old people living independent lives in their own homes as long as they can maintain a satisfactory standard of living there, and that they should be encouraged to make reasonable efforts to do so. Ability to remain independent, or largely so, can often be prolonged if they can be persuaded to shed some of the load of living, for example by moving to a smaller house or flat, or by accepting some supporting services provided by public or voluntary bodies. These services usually concentrate on obvious physical needs such as domestic service and meals, but from what is known of the changes of ability with age, help with problems which loom as complex or confusing, such as interpreting tax and rate forms or arranging and supervising repairs to the house, would often be even more valuable.

To many old people, however, the time comes eventually when independent life is no longer possible. When this happens there are usually only two practical alternatives: either living with younger relatives or moving into an old people's community or home. It would be inappropriate here to try to go fully into the controversial question of which is to be preferred. It is, however, fair to urge that, since the pattern of capacities changes with age and incorporates experience accumulated during life, old people will often differ from those of middle age in their techniques, values and approaches to many facets of living. As a result, coordination of effort between generations in a house is not easily attained, so that the best intentioned efforts by an old person to give help in the home of a married son or daughter are seldom wholly successful and severe social tensions frequently develop.

Far preferable on most grounds for all concerned, and more in line with the implications of the way capacities change with age, is residence in a well-appointed old people's community. Perhaps the ideal is to be found in some of the Australian communities which provide a range of accommodation all the way from flats in which residents are almost completely independent, to full hospital care, with easy transit both ways between one type and another. In this way supporting services can be adjusted to allow the maximum exercise of an older person's abilities without risk of their falling into a state of neglect or reducing relatives to drudgery.

Our discussion throughout this section has been of average trends in old age, but it must be realized that these conceal many individuals whose performance deviates markedly from the general run. In the experiments which my colleagues and I undertook during the decade after the Second World War, we almost always found one or two subjects in their 60s or beyond whose performance was at least as good as the average of those in their 20s. Usually it was only in one or two types of performance that any one person was outstanding, indicating that particular facets of capacity change at different rates within the same individual.

Undue attention to exceptional older people prominent in public life has, in the past, distorted the attitudes of many to the capabilities and needs of old age. On the other hand, it does seem likely that many old people possess unrecognized potentialities for work or leisure activity which could be brought to light if diligently sought. The problem of realizing these potentialities lies more in personality and circumstances than in sheer capacity.

INFORMATIVE READING LISTS

The titles under the first six headings below are well-known and favorably regarded in the field of human development. They represent a broad selection of texts and general books relevant to *The Seven Ages of Man*, and most of them can be read with profit and pleasure by any reader who has enjoyed sections of this book. A few handbook and research monograph titles have been included for the sake of students who want to know where to go next for research reports and bibliographies in areas of their special interests; these are labelled (Tech.). Titles listed under the seventh heading, *Life histories*, are biographies—mostly psychological—that illustrate important aspects of development and methods of case study.

1. Physical development.

Tanner, J. M. *Growth at Adolescence*. (Second edition). Oxford: Blackwell Scientific Publications, 1962.
A thorough review of research on physical changes associated with pubescence and the growth spurt.

2. Personality development.

Bandura, A. & Walters, R. *Social Learning and Personality Development.* New York: Holt, Rinehart and Winston, 1963.
The standard reference on imitation and modelling as processes contributing to the development of personality; technically impeccable but very readable.

Bowlby, J. *Attachment and Loss: I. Attachment.* New York: Basic Books, 1969.
The basic account of how love and attachment to parents develop during the first years of life.

Erikson, E. H. *Childhood and Society.* (Second edition). New York: Norton, 1963.
The classical psychoanalytic study of the development of personality in its cross-cultural context. Especially good on the earlier years.

Lidz, T. *The Person.* New York: Basic Books, 1968.
A clear and very readable account of personality development from birth to death, by a psychoanalytically oriented psychiatrist. It covers in greater detail and with many case vignettes the matters discussed by the present book in the Personality sections. Strongly recommended for any reader who wants to gain a sophisticated understanding of motivation and psychodynamics as these develop through the life cycle.

3. Abilities.

Ginsburg, H. and Opper, S. *Piaget's Theory of Intellectual Development.* New York: Prentice-Hall, 1969.
A clear, concise and readable account of Piaget's theory and description of changes in children's cognitive processes from birth through adolescence.

Sears, P. S. *Intellectual Development.* New York: Wiley, 1971.
A compendium of 32 major theoretical and research articles by leading scholars. Some are classical but most are modern (Tech.).

Terman, L. M. & Oden, M. *The Gifted Group at Mid-Life.* Stanford, Calif.: Stanford University Press, 1959.
This reports the 35-year follow-up of nearly 1500 gifted California children studied since 1921. Contains a full review of previously reported findings on the group, as well as the mid-life data.

4. Textbooks and handbooks.

Brown, R. *Social Psychology.* New York: Free Press, 1965.
A highly readable text on the developmental aspects of children and adults, with special attention to language, intelligence à la Piaget, moral development and group dynamics.

Ferguson, L. R. *Personality Development.* Belmont, Calif.: Brooks-Cole, 1970.
A slender but quite complete paperback volume covering motivational and emotional development from birth into middle adolescence.

McCandless, B. *Adolescence.* Hinsdale, Ill.: Dryden Press, 1970.
A definitive textbook on all aspects of adolescent development.

Mussen, P. H. (Ed.). *Carmichael's Handbook of Child Development.* (Third edition). New York: Wiley, 1970. Two volumes. The standard handbook of research and theory on nearly every aspect of human development, learning, cognition, language, abilities, aggression, attachment and dependency, sex typing, and moral development. Extensive bibliographies. (Tech.).

Mussen, P. H., Conger, J. J. & Kagan, J. *Child Development and Personality.* (Third edition). New York: Harper & Row, 1969.
A standard and very complete text, providing strong supplementation to the present book in the areas of personality and ability—but only through adolescence.

5. Cross-cultural reports.

Bronfenbrenner, U. *Two Worlds of Childhood.* New York: Russell Sage Foundation, 1970.
A comparison of child-rearing policies in the U.S. and U.S.S.R., with suggestions as to how each culture could gain by attending to some of the policies of the other.

Minturn, L. and Lambert, W. W. *Mothers of Six Cultures.* New York: Wiley, 1964.
A comparative study of child-rearing practices and family organization in six widely differing cultures.

Rabin, A. I. *Growing up in the Kibbutz.* New York: Springer, 1965.
A fascinating account of communal child-rearing and its effects on the development of personality and social behavior.

Whiting, J. W. M. and Child, I. L. *Child Training and Personality.* New Haven: Yale University Press, 1953.

The classical cross-cultural study showing the linkage between early experiences and the nature of cultural belief systems, especially those relating to causes of illness.

6. Special topics.

Brown, R. *Words and Things.* New York: Free Press, 1958.
    A charming and detailed account of children's language development, illustrating their early discovery of syntax and other attributes.

Coopersmith, S. *The Antecedents of Self-Esteem.* San Francisco: W. H. Freeman, 1967.
    A readable research report on experiences that influence self-esteem in school age boys.

Erikson, E. H. *Identity: Youth and Crisis.* New York: Norton, 1968.
    A sensitive and comprehensive account of identity crises in adolescence, and the conflict-filled process of passage from adolescence to young adulthood.

Kagan, J. & Moss, H. A. *From Birth to Maturity.* New York: Wiley, 1962.
    A research monograph describing the personality development of the subjects in the famous Fels Institute study. Significant for the first 3 decades of life (Tech.).

Maccoby, E. E. (Ed.) *The Development of Sex Differences.* Stanford, Calif.: Stanford Univ. Press, 1966. A symposium by psychologists, psychiatrists, a sociologist and an anthropologist providing basic data for the understanding of gender role development. (Tech.).

Schacter, S. *The Psychology of Affiliation.* Stanford: Stanford Univ. Press, 1959.
    A series of interesting research studies showing the influence of sibling position in the family on an important personality quality.

Sears, R. R., Maccoby, E. E. & Levin, H. *Patterns of Child Rearing.* New York: Harper and Row, 1957.
    A detailed description of American child rearing practices in the immediate post-World War II era.

Sutton-Smith, B., and Rosenberg, B. G. *The Sibling.* New York: Holt, Rinehart & Winston, 1970. A review of research on the effects of sibling position.

7. Life histories.

Cody, J. *After Great Pain.* Cambridge: Harvard University Press, 1971.
    A psychoanalytic biography of Emily Dickinson's psychosexual development from infancy to later maturity. A brilliant use of personal

documents, together with symbolic interpretation of the poems, to reveal the complexities of her motives and feelings and the defenses she used for coping with them.

Erikson, E. H. *Young Man Luther.* New York: Norton, 1958.
An analytic study illustrating some significant father-son problems in development during young adulthood.

Frank, Anne. *Diary of a Young Girl.* New York: Doubleday, 1952.
A sensitive account of the thoughts and feelings of an adolescent girl, during three critical years, illustrating the normal development under extraordinary wartime conditions.

Freud, S. *Leonardo da Vinci.* (1910). New York: Random House, 1961. Vintage Book, V-132.
The first psychoanalytic study of an artist's psychosexual development; based on biographical information and interpretation of symbols in certain paintings.

Hill, H. *Mark Twain: God's Fool.* New York: Harper & Row, 1973.
A detailed study of Mark Twain's last decade, (age 65 to 75) showing the gradual deterioration of his personality, and illustrating the problems posed by grief and loneliness.

McCurdy, H. T. *The Personality of Shakespeare.* New Haven: Yale University Press, 1953.
A content analysis of the plays is used to reveal changes in the dramatist's motives and interests through the several decades of his adult life.

Salinger, J. D. *The Catcher in the Rye.* Boston: Little, Brown, 1951.
A sensitive fictional account of an adolescent's search for identity.

INDEX